A. P. Giannini
and the
Bank of America

THE OKLAHOMA WESTERN BIOGRAPHIES
RICHARD W. ETULAIN, GENERAL EDITOR

A. P. Giannini

and the

Bank of America

By Gerald D. Nash

UNIVERSITY OF OKLAHOMA PRESS : NORMAN AND LONDON

Other Books by Gerald D. Nash

*State Government and Economic Development: A History of Administrative
Policies in California, 1849–1933* (Berkeley, 1964; New York, 1978)
Issues in American Economic History (ed.) (Boston, 1964, 1972, 1980)
Franklin Delano Roosevelt (ed.) (Englewood Cliffs, 1967)
*United States Oil Policy, 1890–1964: Business and Government in Twentieth-
Century America* (Pittsburgh, 1968; Westport, Conn., 1976)
Perspectives on Administration: The Vistas of History (Berkeley, 1969)
The Great Transition: A Short History of Twentieth-Century America
(Boston, 1971)
*The American West in the Twentieth Century: A Short History of an Urban
Oasis* (Englewood Cliffs, 1973; Albuquerque, 1977)
The Great Depression and World War II (New York, 1979, 1992)
Social Security: The First Half-Century (ed.) (with Noel Pugach and
Richard F. Tomasson) (Albuquerque, 1988)
The Twentieth Century West: Historical Interpretations (ed.) (with Richard
W. Etulain) (Albuquerque, 1989)
The American West Transformed: The Impact of the Second World War
(Bloomington, Ind., 1985; Lincoln, Nebr., 1990)
Creating the West: Historical Interpretations, 1890–1990 (Albuquerque, 1991)
World War II and the West: Reshaping the Economy (Lincoln, Nebr., 1990)

Library of Congress Cataloging-in-Publication Data

Nash, Gerald D.
    A.P. Giannini and the Bank of America / by Gerald D. Nash.—1st
ed.
        p.   cm.—(The Oklahoma western biographies ; v. 5)
    Includes bibliographical references and index.
    ISBN 0-8061-2461-X
    1. Giannini, Amadeo Peter, 1870–1949.   2. Bankers—United States—
Biography.   3. Bank of America—History.   4. Banks and banking—
West (U.S.)—History.   I. Title.   II. Series.
HG2463.G5N37   1992
332.1'23'0973—dc20   92-54131
                                                                                    CIP

A. P. Giannini and the Bank of America is Volume 5 of The Oklahoma Western
Biographies.

The paper in this book meets the guidelines for permanence and durability
of the Committee on Production Guidelines for Book Longevity of the
Council on Library Resources, Inc. ∞

Contents

Illustrations

Series Editor's Preface

AMADEO Peter Giannini (1870–1949) grew up with the American West. As Gerald Nash's illuminating biography reveals, A. P.'s career paralleled California's transformation from a promising periphery at the end of the nineteenth century into a powerful economic core by the midtwentieth century. At the same time that the Pacific Slope gradually emerged as the leading subregion of the West, A. P. established and directed a bank that mushroomed into a powerful global institution by his death.

In steady, clear strokes, Nash limns Giannini's dramatic rise to power. The son of an Italian immigrant farmer/rancher, A. P. early demonstrated his ambition, diligence, and frugality. Recognizing the restrictive and sometimes selfish policies of earlier bankers, Giannini focused his attentions and energies on ordinary citizen investors. Concerned with what he called "the little fellow," A. P. directed his Bank of Italy and later the mammoth Bank of America to pay special heed to their needs. As a result, he democratized an entire economic field through pioneering branch banking. As early as 1909, Giannini opened a branch outside San Francisco. By the early 1920s an expanding web of more than sixty branches served customers from Chico to San Diego.

Always a quick study, Giannini continued to innovate throughout his active career. Operating on the philosophy that money must never lie idle, he made the resources of his sprawling bank available to large businesses, the federal government, and even movie moguls, while simultaneously catering to wage earners, small investors, and home builders. Thoughtful, observant, and energetic, A. P. was both idealistic and opportunistic, twin impulses that impelled the Bank of America forward to become one of the world's largest banks by the late 1940s.

While narrating this intriguing success story, Nash does not overlook his subject's blemishes and limitations. Often impatient with competitors and with bank workers with whom he disagreed, Giannini frequently coerced employees to march to his drumbeat or drop out of his band. At times his monumental self-assurance, his driving ambition, and his dogmatism alienated his friends—and even family members. Nash's coverage of these character flaws is particularly revealing and balanced.

Giannini's story is also based on thorough research in a variety of published and manuscript sources. Adeptly marshaling these materials, Nash, more than any other biographer, demonstrates A. P.'s central role in the economic development of the American West. As the best recent account of Giannini, this solid, readable biography adds to Gerald Nash's notable reputation as a leading interpreter of the twentieth-century American West even as it details the career of one of the region's most influential citizens.

RICHARD W. ETULAIN

University of New Mexico

Preface

IN this book I present a brief profile of A. P. Giannini. My aim is to explain in clear, nontechnical terms why and how he succeeded as he did, and how his life affected the West during the first half of the twentieth century. My focus is not on the history of the bank. Nor have I attempted a detailed scholarly biography, a task that still remains to be accomplished. Rather, I have tried to provide an interpretive study that will convey to the reader a better understanding of a remarkable man and of his impact on the West.

In the preparation of this book I received help from a wide range of individuals. My first forays into the subject were made more than thirty years ago, when Russell Posner proved to be a superb guide. Over the years I have also benefited from the advice of Vincent P. Carosso of New York University, one of the undisputed authorities on American banking history. The editor of this series, Richard W. Etulain, provided unfailing encouragement, wisdom, and advice. The library staff at the University of Göttingen in Germany, where I served as George Bancroft Professor of American History during 1990–91 and where I completed this study, were consistently patient and resourceful with an American who seemed to have unusual requests. My wife, Marie, eased labors on the manuscript. All of these individuals helped to improve the study, but I alone am responsible for errors and omissions.

GERALD D. NASH

Albuquerque, N.M.

A. P. Giannini
and the
Bank of America

Introduction

THIS is the story of the West's leading banker in the twentieth century. Yet it is not really so much the story of a banker as it is the tale of a dreamer, or of a man who relentlessly and often ruthlessly pursued the American Dream and found realization and self-fulfillment in it. The son of immigrants, Amadeo Peter Giannini—A. P. to everyone—found an environment in California and the West that enabled him to bring many of his dreams to fruition. California at the turn of the century was still an undeveloped country. It provided fertile ground for individuals with ambitions on a giant scale, which matched the dimensions of the land in which they found themselves. In history men and women are not always well matched with the times, the cultures, and the societies in which they find themselves. But in A. P.'s case, the fit was close. Here was a restless, bold, and imaginative personality who flourished in an unspoiled and underdeveloped environment that provided him with a vast arena for expressing his talents.

In many ways the Bank of America was an extension of A. P.'s personality. Clearly, the institution that he built became too complex to rely on the existence of a single man. But such was the force of his personality that he left his imprint on the bank's orientation and on its policies for the next generation. And when after 1980 new hands at the wheel swerved from the course he had set, they brought the Bank of America to the brink of collapse. Certainly many of the banking practices successful in the first half of the twentieth century were no longer as relevant in the changed economic environment of succeeding decades. But his vision of an institution that would cater to a mass market still retained validity.

During his lifetime, however, A. P. dominated the Bank of America as no other single individual did. It made little difference what particular title he held—his was always the final word. It was he who had the insight to recognize the potentials of a mass market.

He had a remarkable understanding of the psychological needs and wants of the average person. He himself was an uncommon individual who had the common touch. He had vision and imagination, which allowed him to anticipate the future effectively. He knew how to delegate authority, to centralize as well as decentralize a sprawling organization, to motivate his staff, and to administer punishments and rewards. He was not always an easy taskmaster, but often an effective one. His entrepreneurial instincts were unusually accurate, his appetite for new enterprises unlimited. To him the extension of branch banking was a great adventure. It was his very life and being. Even when he was presiding over a multibillion dollar banking empire encompassing more than six hundred banks, he could still get excited about the opening of a new branch in a tiny community of fewer than a thousand souls. It was the central focus of his life, and he never lost his relish for it. He had the eye of the hunter for new prey—in his case, financial institutions. In him, atavism was transformed into entrepreneurship.

A biography about a major figure in the twentieth-century West is particularly timely because in the last two decades various writers— mostly of a journalistic bent—have placed an undue emphasis on destructive elements in the development of the West. In a distinctly present-minded mood they have pointed to the spoliation of the environment; to the suppression of women, minorities, and native peoples; and to what they regard as wanton exploitation of people and resources by large corporations. To some extent such complaints may be justified. Unfortunately, such a one-dimensional view reads too much of the present into the past. It distorts the history of the region as much as those romanticized versions of western history that found an unbroken record of peace and progress. The development of the twentieth-century West contained both elements—destruction as well as building. Obviously, Giannini was a builder, a gifted architect of the West's largest bank, who, by providing needed services, contributed greatly to the region's growth. He also could be ruthless and exploitative. In fact, he never quite understood the fears of those who viewed him as a monopolist and who opposed his efforts to build a highly centralized bank on a national scale. As A. P.'s life illustrates, the economic development of the twentieth-century West was not an abstract or impersonal process but a very human enterprise.

CHAPTER 1

A Bank Is Born, 1870–1905

THE earth shook and trembled on that fateful Wednesday in San Francisco on April 18, 1906, one that city dwellers there long remembered. That day witnessed the city's great earthquake, which itself inspired great fear and trepidation. But worse was to follow after the first initial shocks. Within a few hours, broken gas lines produced a spate of fires. Soon whole neighborhoods were ablaze. For days the skies seemed aglow with an eerie red, and large black clouds of smoke rose on the horizon. Both human and animal panicked in this raging inferno. People screamed as they scurried, and everywhere fire engines and bucket brigades added to an almost surrealistic atmosphere of confusion. Finally, after four days, the fires gradually subsided. Black embers glowed among the rubble that had been buildings just a few days before. San Franciscans who lived through those eventful nights remembered scenes that could have come out of Dante's hell.

But amid this atmosphere of ruin and desolation, one could espy a tall, determined figure, calm and deliberate, patiently riding in what appeared like a produce wagon pulled by slow and placid mares. In the dark twilight he appeared like a ghostly shadow, wending his way slowly through the crush of carts and wagons that crowded the roads out of San Francisco. Although surrounded by the tumult of his unusual surroundings, he seemed to stand out as one who clearly knew his way.

The man in question was A. P. Giannini, a young banker then thirty-five years of age. In many respects, this brief episode in his life characterized much of his whole career. Amid the chaos and turbulence of daily events that swept about him, he always retained his sense of destiny, always remained a man with a mission. That mission, to which he was fiercely devoted all his life, was to contribute to and participate in the economic development of his native state of California, as entrepreneur, business manager, and banker. And eventually he extended his ambitions to embrace the entire nation and even the world.

When A. P. was born in 1870, California was just emerging from the gold rush era. For centuries it had been a languid land dotted by Spanish, and then Mexican, rancheros—a thinly populated area dotted by large cattle ranches and coastal missions. Its Indian population had been declining steadily since the arrival of whites, decimated by disease and cruel exploitation. But the gold rush of 1849 disrupted this placid civilization. Within a decade it brought more than 100,000 people to the new state. And even as the search for gold began to wane in 1860, still others poured in, attracted by lush lands and tempting opportunities in farming, business, commerce, and finance. These endeavors, rather than mining, came to be the great attractions for the newcomers of the 1860s. During that decade land speculators also laid the foundations for large-scale commercial agriculture, the agribusiness of the future. By 1872 Henry George, the famous reformer and advocate of the single tax, was crying out against the land monopolization of his day. With anguish he witnessed the waning of the Jeffersonian dream, of a society of small, self-sufficient farmers in California. Although some opportunities for small-scale farming developed, corporate agriculture became increasingly dominant. But whether large or small, California's varied enterprises multiplied rapidly. The pace of economic growth surged rapidly between 1865 and 1869 as the completion of the transcontinental railroad brought another large influx of new migrants. By 1870 the population had grown to 560,000.

Into this exciting and dynamic environment A. P. was born in San Jose on May 6, 1870. In later years he remembered his early youth with great affection, for he felt that its atmosphere had done much to mold his later life. "San Jose had a population of about fourteen thousand," he recalled as an adult. "It was located in the Santa Clara Valley about fifty miles from San Francisco. Back in the days of the gold rush, it had been a pretty rough town. But then things settled down and families began moving in to build small cottages and buy land on which to farm. On our own farm in Alviso, just outside San Jose, we grew lots of different kinds of fruits and vegetables— specialty crops mostly, like artichokes and strawberries. I didn't care very much for farming, but it is sincere, honest work, which is the best recipe for happiness I know."

A. P. sprang from recently arrived Italian immigrants. His father,

Luigi, was a poor, robust peasant, a twenty-two-year-old settler from Chavari, Italy, a remote mountain village about forty miles from Genoa. Luigi had first come to California in 1864 in search of gold but was quickly disappointed. Yet he was greatly impressed by the California countryside and the climate, since it seemed familiar to an Italian from a Mediterranean environment. Like many of his countrymen, he dreamed of settling down on a small farm of his own some day and carefully saved money earned from odd jobs. One day in the early spring of 1869, Luigi was sitting around a campfire with his compatriots, including two brothers from Chavari, who excitedly read a letter aloud from their youngest sister, Virginia De Martini.

Several decades later Virginia's sister, Theresa, recalled the incident. "Luigi was friend of my brothers," she noted. "Being friendly, they often discussed the news that came from Italy, and they were in the habit of reading together the letters that my sister Virginia used to write my brothers. Virginia's style of letter writing revealed many of her good qualities and a lively sense of energy. Luigi was so impressed that he secretly left California for Italy to woo and marry her. To impress her parents, he carried a money belt with an ample supply of $20 gold pieces." After a month of frenzied courtship Luigi married Virginia in Chavari on August 10, 1869, shortly after her fifteenth birthday. "It was the most exciting celebration we had ever seen," Virginia's sister remembered. "Virginia wore a white hat to the wedding, a gift from Luigi from America. The hat attracted much attention among the wedding guests. They had never seen one before. Italian women did not wear them." Soon thereafter, in October 1869, Luigi and his new wife left for New York on a sailing ship and then took the new transcontinental railroad to San Jose. They arrived in the midst of a frenzied real estate boom there.

Like most newcomers, the young couple sought out fellow immigrants in the city. In fact, most of the ten thousand people there had arrived only recently. Many of them were Italians attracted especially by the vineyards of the Santa Clara Valley. Upon arrival, Luigi decided to lease the Swiss Hotel, a twenty-room structure, of which he became proprietor. It was there that A. P. was born. Like many peasants, however, Luigi longed to own a piece of land. During his first twelve months in the hotel business, he was able to save enough money to buy a tract of forty acres near Alviso, a suburb of San Jose. Between 1871 and 1876 he farmed this land quite successfully, meanwhile learning English and acquiring U.S. citizenship. During these years he also fathered two other sons: Attilio Henry, born in 1874, and George, who arrived in 1877.

A. P.'s childhood was ordinary and unexceptional. Although his family was not wealthy, they were comfortable and lacked little. As a boy A. P. helped with the many chores that a fruit orchard requires. He picked apricots, strawberries, and cherries, for the valley was one of nature's natural hothouses. His formal education began in a small schoolhouse in San Jose and in a one-room school in Alviso. An impressionable young boy, he learned as much from his surroundings as he did from books. All about him he could see prosperous fruit orchards producing for growing markets in big cities such as San Francisco, and also distant ones like Chicago and New York. By 1875 the great fleets of refrigerator cars owned by the Pacific Fruit Express were carrying the fruits and vegetables of the Santa Clara Valley to every part of the nation. Alviso thus was more than a sleepy country town because its prosperity depended on faraway markets. On most days the hustle and bustle of trade and commerce animated the community. Local farmers brought their wagons loaded with produce to the Alviso landing, where sweating stevedores would load it on steamers bound for San Francisco, unless it moved eastward by rail. As a youngster, A. P. was deeply impressed by the hubbub. Maybe one day he too could be part of this busy scene.

But then, quite unexpectedly, tragedy struck the happy Giannini home. On August 13, 1876, as A. P.'s father was driving his produce wagon in front of their house, he was gunned down by Jose Ferrerra, one of his field workers, over a minor salary dispute. As the six-year-old son looked on in horror, Luigi died almost instantly.

Fortunately, A. P.'s mother proved to be a remarkably resourceful person. Although only twenty-two years old when her husband died, she took over the management of the family farm while raising her three small children. Many times she accompanied the product of her farm on the steamer that carried it to the San Francisco markets. One of these boats was the coastal ship *Reform*, whose captain, John Leale, remembered her as a pleasant and handsome lady. She would sit on the crowded deck quietly, he reminisced, with her small boy, A. P., as the vessel slid through the darkness of the early morning on the chilly bay. When not attending to the sale of her crops, she would head into the town to buy food and various supplies. Sometimes she walked, but on occasion she secured a ride with one of the many teamsters who were hauling fruits and vegetables to Alviso. On one of these trips she met Lorenzo Scatena, a twenty-six-year-old Italian immigrant who had come to San Jose in 1863 and who worked as a driver for the San Francisco commission house of Onesti and Connor. Mrs. Giannini sold much of her produce to the firm. Soon she and Scatena became good friends, and in June of 1880 they were married. Scatena moved to the Giannini farm and took over some of the heaviest chores while still continuing in his job as hauler.

A. P.'s home life therefore remained stable. When he reflected on this phase of his youth as an adult, A. P. remembered fondly his schooling and his friends. "At school I studied with children of many nationalities," he declared—"Portuguese, French, German, Armenian, Spanish, Japanese, and Americans. Unable to pronounce my Italian name, they called me 'Amador Jenning,' which didn't bother me at all. I had a good time at school, learning as quickly as any of the pupils and establishing friendships which endured through life. In the afternoon, when the weather was warm, I swam with the boys in the Guadalupe slough, a few hundred yards west of the school grounds. . . . What with mud churned up by the boats and water washed down from the canneries that crunched and steamed so odorously on the shore of the bay, the swimming was not the best, but we didn't pay much attention to the disadvantages."

As A. P. entered adolescence, he found his small world expanding. Lorenzo adopted the three sons of his wife and provided them with a strong father image. He had three more children with Virginia: Henry, Florence, and Pearl. The unsettled economic conditions in California near the end of the 1870s made the farm far less prosperous than in former years; however, Lorenzo looked about for other opportunities to support his growing family. A. P.'s mother was ambitious for them all and prevailed upon her new husband to leave the farm and instead enter the commission business in San Jose. They moved there in 1879, and three years later to San Francisco, where there were greater opportunities. Moreover, A. P.'s mother appreciated the superior schools of a large city. Urban life meant some changes for the Giannini household. Their first home was a rented one on Jackson Street, not far from San Francisco's Barbary Coast. Lorenzo Scatena now went to work as a trader for the produce commission firm of A. Galli and Sons. His job was to act as a middleman between the growers of fruits and vegetables, on the one hand, and San Francisco fruit stores and restaurants, on the other. It was hard and demanding work. He would examine the produce as it arrived on the docks in the wee hours of the morning, usually at 1:00 or 2:00 A.M. This required an acute, sure sense of judgment because a trader was obliged to sell the merchandise very quickly, within a few hours, by auction, contract, or simple haggling, in view of its perishable nature.

Scatena showed a great aptitude for his new job. Usually he worked at least sixteen hours daily, from midnight until the next afternoon. Only then would he return home for a few hours of sleep and a warm meal. As Scatena later recalled: "Those were the days when it was necessary for us to get to work early to buy, sell, and handle our produce. If we did not get down there early, we could not sell, and we would have lost the produce we had bought. We left home at midnight; 1:00 A.M. was a late hour—often too late—to show up on the docks." As an impressionable teenager, A. P. thus grew up observing the hectic routine of his stepfather. He became increasingly familiar with the intricacies of the fruit commission business, much of which was in the hands of Italian-Americans.

Lorenzo Scatena quickly became a role model for his ambitious young son. After his first successful year in the new profession, Scatena decided to go into business on his own. For the first time in his life his annual income reached five figures, and he was able to move his family to a handsome new house at 411 Green Street in San Francisco. This was in the city's North Beach district, which was rapidly becoming the hub of the city's Italian community. There he provided a stable home for the Giannini clan as he prospered increasingly during the next decade.

Although he attended the nearby Washington Grammar School, from the time he was twelve years old A. P. became more and more fascinated by the commission business. Before and after school he would follow "Pop" Scatena around, observing his dealings with farmers and retail merchants. Every day seemed to present new challenges and excitements. A. P. soon found himself riveted much more to his father's business dealings than to his schoolbooks. Despite the protests of his mother, he would often sneak away from home at midnight to follow his father on the way to work and would observe Lorenzo's bargaining on the docks throughout the night. Only in the early morning hours would A. P. rush off to a small restaurant for breakfast, before going on to school. His sleeping time was irregular, to say the least. Catching a few winks after school, he would be back in his father's office by later afternoon, watching and listening to the flow of transactions. After an early supper he would sleep some more until midnight, when the next round of excitement started up again.

In this developing regimen, A. P.'s formal schooling clearly became less relevant. His interests in class were concentrated on penmanship and arithmetic, both subjects which had an immediate practical application in business. His grades in school were quite good, but in his mind they were just secondary. As he noted in later years, he might have become the best student in his class, "but for a little trouble with the teacher. Working around my stepfather's commission business I learned to write pretty well. Whenever there was a chance to uphold the honors of the class, I was sent to the blackboard to write. That put me on the honorary list, but someone began calling me 'teacher's pet,' and I refused to write any more. I did not have to take examinations to pass, but my stubbornness lost the laurels."

Personal temperament, therefore, as well as home environment turned A. P. to a business career in his early teens. Clearly, he preferred to turn his intelligence and learning to practical ends. While watching his father on the docks, he developed the practice of copying ship manifests of vessels bringing in the produce. These notations provided Scatena with extensive data about each day's consignments. Most of his competitors had only vague ideas about just how much produce was available on a given day. At the same time, the young teenager began soliciting new business. On most days he went to his father's office after school and would write dozens of letters to farmers in the San Francisco area, offering to sell their crops on consignment at fair and honest prices. This was A. P.'s first major business venture, and it proved to be remarkably successful in attracting new customers to the firm.

Meanwhile, his mother became increasingly concerned about his preoccupation with business and his lack of enthusiasm for school. She also worried about his health, particularly because of his lack of sleep. Like many immigrant Americans, she had the hope that her sons might graduate from high school, or perhaps even college. Unfortunately, A. P. was clearly not oriented in that direction. When A. P. was not yet quite fifteen, Mrs. Giannini persuaded her husband to discourage his son's intense interest in business. Hoping to impress upon A. P. some of the difficulties of the commission trade, Scatena offered him a gold watch for the first carload of oranges he could buy from a grower who was not a customer of the firm. He considered such a feat impossible because at the time oranges were considered luxuries in the San Francisco produce trade and difficult to secure. Yet three weeks later A. P. walked in on his father with a consignment order, not for one, but for two boxcars of oranges from the Santa Ana Fruit Company in Tustin. "I still have the gold watch Pop Scatena gave me for the letter that brought that business," A. P. recalled proudly when he was an adult. "It reminds me that the only pleasure I had and the only pleasure I ever wanted as a young boy was the reward and pleasure of a successful transaction." He could have added that such motivation came to be the driving force for much of his life.

Instead of discouraging A. P. in his fascination with business, this experience only spurred him on. In the late spring of 1885 he decided that he wanted to drop out of school so that he could devote himself more fully to the affairs of Scatena's firm. "I decided school had nothing more to offer me," A. P. told an interviewer in later years. "I wanted to get ahead. I studied the matter carefully in my mind and then acted." This was just a month before his scheduled graduation from the eighth grade. His mother was crushed. To please her, A. P. agreed to enroll in a three-month course in accounting at Heald's Business School in San Francisco. With deliberate speed he completed the work in six weeks and then hurried back to Scatena's firm to get on with business at the waterfront. "It was ambition, I guess," A. P. reflected later. "I wanted to get ahead. That was the kind of work I wanted to do. There wasn't any sense in putting it off."

A. P. now threw himself into full-time work in the commission business with great energy and passion. He liked nothing better than to submerge himself in the milling crowds along the waterfront, rubbing shoulders with stevedores, teamsters, farmers, and merchants. Here was a microcosm of humanity, including Chinese, Levantines, Irish, Russians, Romanians, and, most frequently, Italians. A. P. loved to fraternize with this throng, relishing the familiar faces he saw nightly. This became his life. At fifteen years of age he became entry clerk and salesman for his father's company. He would be on the docks by 11:00 P.M., making deals until early next morning. Then he would rush off to the office to handle necessary correspondence and to write scores of letters to solicit new customers. He was growing up fast. By now he had grown to a little over six feet tall, with a heavy muscular build and a shock of thick black hair. Full of energy, his job was his most vital passion. One of his competitors, George Webster, discussed his success: "I've seen men go up to him, after having rehearsed to themselves plausible reasons why they should buy beans, let us say, at three cents a pound under his price; but before the story ever stumbled past their lips, they would be signing their names to an order at his figure, which was probably a perfectly fair one."

Within a few months his pent-up energies led him to extend his range of activities. Before the end of 1885 he began to accompany his father as he went on purchasing trips into the agricultural areas of the Sacramento Valley. During these years developers and farmers were rapidly settling the interior areas of California, and many of the leading commission merchants in San Francisco were hiring salespeople to solicit business in the newer regions. Since the Sacramento River provided cheap and rapid access for shipping goods to the coast, A. P. savored the opportunities he saw about him and threw himself into the new challenge with great enthusiasm. Scouring the area by horse and buggy, often working more than eighteen hours daily, visiting dozens of produce farmers along the river, he bought hundreds of tons of cantaloupes, pears, cherries, plums, grapes, beans, and potatoes each week. Rarely taking time out for meals, he would munch on cheese and crackers while he was on the road to see new clients. Unlike others at his age, he spurned rest and relaxation. "I kept working hard sticking to business," he remembered in later years, "and not paying attention to anything else like hanging around with the boys and going to parties and dances. I decided what I wanted and then went after it hammer and tongs." With each customer he stayed only long enough to write out business agreements, after some initial pleasantries. A very congenial young man, he rarely forgot names and would ask clients about their health, their wives, and their children. But business was business, and he was always anxious to get on his way. Yet he exuded an amiable image and impressed people by his integrity, earnestness, and fair dealing. His first trips were a great success and only whetted his desire to build the commission firm of Scatena into the largest in the city.

During the next two years A. P. broadened his activities and extended his territory to include the Napa and Santa Clara valleys. Always an avid talker, he would ride his horse into the surrounding countryside to talk with farmers about their business affairs, the upcoming season, and market prospects. "His curiosity about local conditions was insatiable," one of his friends observed. "He never tired of stopping strangers on the streets and back roads of remote farm towns to ask question after question, absorbing as much information about the place as he possibly could." He also inspired confidence in those with whom he dealt and soon advised many of the growers on how to shape their plans for a profitable season. Since he was away from San Francisco for weeks at a time, he lived in boarding houses at night and traveled by any means available, including horseback, stagecoach, or riverboat. Sometimes he simply walked. He also visited farms considered too remote by his competitors and made his way across roads, even when they were flooded or otherwise impassable. As A. P. noted: "I had my own ideas how a commission house should be run. The ideas were different from those of others in the trade. Mine were sound, and they won."

A. P. soon became the talk of his competitors. His single-mindedness became legendary. As A. P. himself admitted: "I always came to the point just as quickly as I decently could. I wasn't a bit interested in anything whatsoever not connected with my business. I had a clear object in view, and I went after that object as straight as I knew how. I have never believed in beating around the bush." Although he sometimes incurred hostility from his rivals, that did not dissuade him from seeking to beat them in a deal. In one incident in 1886, he was traveling to the house of one of his largest customers when he espied one of his competitors driving his buggy to the same place. But A. P. remembered a possible shortcut to the ranch. So he tied his horse to a tree, swam across a slough while holding his clothes above his head, and, after drying himself, ran breathlessly to the farmer's residence. There he was filling out the papers for the coveted transaction when his competitor finally arrived, having taken the long way around the water's edge. As one of his contemporaries noted: "He never let anyone take a customer away from him if he could help it. Salesmanship of that sort just gets under your skin."

A. P. stalked his prospects as if they were prey. The story was told of his efforts to secure the account of R. W. Eaton of Watsonville, who was reputed to grow some of the finest fruit in the state. When first approached by A. P., Eaton was hesitant and wondered why he should switch his satisfactory arrangements with another company. A. P. made numerous trips to see Eaton, tried all of his powers of persuasion, yet had little success. Then he tried a different approach. One Sunday morning A. P. sat down on Eaton's doorstep and then followed him to church. At the choir door Eaton informed A. P. that he was going up to the choir and that he certainly did not care to discuss a business contract on a Sunday. But A. P. followed him up the stairs and sat down at his side. With that, Eaton finally caved in. "You can have the contract," he is reputed to have said, "if you will just let me alone."

A. P.'s phenomenal performance did much to expand the size of Scatena's firm. By the time he was nineteen years old, his father offered him a one-third partnership. Two years later Scatena gave him a half-interest. Meanwhile, A. P. began to expand the range of the company's operations, offering his customers advances and small loans. Farmers frequently needed small amounts of cash for a variety of purposes or to tide them over a slow season. A. P. understood their situation and was happy to oblige. Usually he based his lending policies on a person's character, trusting to the soundness of his judgment. More often than not, he was right. In these early years he thus developed increasing confidence in the accuracy of his appraisal of particular business situations. Although he would usually charge low interest for such loans, sometimes he asked for nothing, hoping to attach a client more closely to the firm. In addition, he did much to extend the geographic range of the company's operations. When the coming of the Santa Fe Railroad in 1887 inaugurated a boom in Los Angeles and southern California, A. P. immediately saw new opportunities for exploitation. Within a year he was actively soliciting new accounts there. He was especially impressed by the potentials of the little hamlet of Hollywood, at the time just a sea of orange groves.

By the time he was twenty-one A. P. had already developed many of the qualities that characterized him during his business career. When George Webster, a friend, was once asked why A. P. was so successful, he replied: "I'll be hanged if I know. Perhaps because he could convince a customer that his best chances lay in trusting. . . . There was a psychological something about his self-confidence, an uncanny accuracy in his foresight, an inevitability in his methods, that had us licked before we started fighting. . . . I don't think he ever lost an account or a contest of any kind. No such salesman was ever encountered before on the waterfront. No one could bluff, intimidate, or outgeneral him. In those price wars over perishable commodities, which sometimes meant sharp temporary losses, A. P. had an extraordinary faculty for gauging how long the other fellow could stand the gaff." A. P. and California were well matched. Both he and the state reflected enormous diversity, optimism, talent, and remarkable energy. The blending of A. P.'s personality with his particular environment seemed uncanny.

Contemporaries also remembered the twenty-one-year-old A. P. as one of the most striking "comers" in the closely knit Italian-American community of North Beach. By now he cut a smart figure. On holidays he would wear a top hat, gloves, and a Prince Albert coat while sporting a handsome cane. Although keeping an exclusive eye on business, he also had keen ambitions in his private life. A propitious marriage could benefit both his public as well as his personal affairs. While attending Mass at the old Spanish church between Mason and Powell streets in San Francisco in 1891, A. P. spotted a pretty young woman in the choir. She was Clorinda Agnes Cuneo, who also happened to be the daughter of one of the wealthiest Italian-Americans in North Beach. Although not literate in English, the elder Cuneo had made a fortune in real estate. A. P. faced an impediment, however, since Clorinda was engaged to a young medical student. But that young man at the time was in Europe to secure graduate training in pediatrics. Never one to be outdone by a rival, A. P. began a deliberate campaign to win her affections. He took her out on picnics, planned trips to theatrical productions, sent flowers and candy in profusion, and wrote a series of ardent love letters. After three months he was successful in winning her hand. Once again, A. P. had bested the competition. On September 12, 1892, he married Clorinda in an elaborate wedding, inaugurating a union that was to last for nearly half a century.

The Gianninis lived comfortably. Initially the newlywed couple moved into a small house near fashionable Russian Hill, just outside the Italian neighborhood of North Beach. Six months later A. P. acquired a small frame house on Green Street near Washington Square in North Beach because it was only a few minutes away from the waterfront, which continued to be a center for A. P.'s life. During their first year of marriage the Gianninis had a son. Two other boys and a daughter completed the circle of their family. Two other children died in infancy. As the family grew, A. P. acquired a very comfortable house in the exclusive San Francisco suburb of Burlingame, about thirty miles to the south on the peninsula, where they resided until they moved to nearby San Mateo, to what became their lifelong home.

Meanwhile, throughout the decade of the 1890s, A. P.'s talents and energy did much to make Scatena and Sons one of the largest and most successful commission merchants in San Francisco. A. P. roamed throughout the entire state, although he concentrated a good portion of his efforts in the orange-growing sections of the south. His strategy quite frequently was to focus special attention on a particular community or group of growers and then to conduct intense campaigns to win their business. His ventures at times resembled military operations, in which A. P., as commanding general, carefully chose targets and worked out a complicated strategy to achieve his objectives. In addition, he provided an extra element of service to his customers, so much that it gave him an edge over most of his competitors in an extremely competitive and difficult business environment. In later years he would reflect many of these same characteristics in the banking field.

During the nineties he also displayed other traits that were to become hallmarks of his style of operation. He had a fierce and intensive competitive streak that was to become his trademark. He simply wanted to be the best in whatever he did, and he drove himself and others relentlessly to achieve his goals. Although he always had a grasp of the big picture, he also had a fine eye for detail. And while he was always intent on earning profits, at the same time he usually tied that aim to the human dimensions of a deal. His psychological perceptions were shrewd.

Many of these qualities were reflected in his business policies, of which the marketing of odd lots of produce in the 1890s can serve as an example. Odd lots usually consisted of one or two crates in a total shipment of three hundred or more. They would often be the results of the efforts of a farmer's wife or one of his children who hoped to earn a little extra cash. A. P.'s customers were often wholesalers, however, who were loath to buy small quantities.

To placate his farmer-suppliers A. P. made special efforts to dispose of these odd lots. While delivering a large order, he would casually add on one or two of these extra crates. If his customer objected, A. P. would gently project an "all or nothing" attitude while his trucks and horses were waiting. Since the sums involved were usually quite small, wholesalers would usually accept the extra box or two, without much grumbling. The policy helped A. P. not only to clear his warehouses but also to please his suppliers.

Despite his success in the commission business (or more accurately, because of it), by the late 1890s A. P. was becoming restless. He had achieved his aim in making Scatena and Sons the largest commission house in San Francisco, with six-figure annual profits. But the firm no longer presented the challenge it had held for him a decade earlier. Since he had met the competition and beat it, life was no longer as interesting. As he broadened his horizons, he began to look for new fields to conquer. For a short time it seemed as if politics might provide an outlet for his nervous energies.

Indeed, early in his career A. P. came to realize the importance of good political connections in the furthering of his business enterprises. In 1899 political corruption was as rife in San Francisco as it was in many other boss-ridden cities of the period. There the dominant boss was Blind Chris Buckley, who had an iron grip on the city's politics, and especially on the forty-fourth Assembly District, which included North Beach. That area embraced not only the homes of many Italian-Americans but also their business enterprises. Buckley's henchmen in the district, men like Deputy Sheriff George Ryan or the secretary of the Fire Commission, George Maxwell, had a tight control over many aspects of life in the neighborhood. They not only solicited bribes but also subjected store owners to shakedowns. In addition, they often intimidated voters. Buying and selling of votes was a common procedure, with the standard rate at about five dollars. Such practices gave the area a bad reputation that made it more difficult to attract investment capital for new forms of business. Moreover, many of the merchants in the neighborhood also found that they had great difficulty in securing bank loans because of the unsavory political situation. Like many business leaders, A. P. was therefore sympathetic to a burgeoning reform movement that was developing in the city. The reformers promised to promote, rather than to inhibit, business activities of all kinds. A great deal of the reform sentiment crystallized around progressive Republicans in California. In San Francisco the leading crusader was James D. Phelan, an able attorney who ran for the mayoralty in 1899 against the corrupt machine candidate of Boss Buckley.

A. P. enthusiastically threw his support behind Phelan, whom he had come to know well. Ordinarily A. P. devoted his entire time to business, but he had come to realize that business and politics were closely intertwined. As he noted in later years: "October and November were quiet months in the commission business. I got into politics because of a desire to help Phelan. It was a diversion. I had lots of energy, and this gave me an outlet. I never got behind a cause, however, unless I thought it was in the best interests of the people as a whole."

A. P. soon threw himself into active management of the campaign. He organized a New Charter Democratic Club to serve as the spearhead of the reformers in the district. At the same time, he rented an entire floor in a three-story building on Union and Powell streets to serve as headquarters. There he put up large signs to announce the formation of the new group. Meanwhile, he spent many evenings meeting with volunteers and local officials to plan strategies. He arranged rallies, secured speakers, and gathered support for delegates to the county Democratic convention. Often too busy with his own business affairs to give minute attention to all necessary details, he secured the services of a respected physician, Dr. L. D. Bacigalupi, to supervise the day-to-day operations of the club. When he could, however, he was out on the streets to shake the hands of Italian voters in the district, among whom he was already well known. He would introduce candidates in either Italian or English and then would provide a sales pitch not very different from what he used in his business transactions. In fact, A. P. viewed the challenge in somewhat similar terms. "We were selling good government," he said. "All the big industrial plants were visited, the iron works, the shipyards and the other places where large bodies of men were employed. I wanted the candidates to meet the voters and to convince them the same way a businessman does to buy goods."

A. P. left little to chance. After supervising his intensive grass roots, door-to-door campaign, he also made sure that the voters would get to the polls. At his own expense he hired seventy-five horses and buggies, together with armed guards, to transport citizens to voting stations and then to return them to their homes. Many people had been afraid to venture out, fearing (with good reason) that Boss Buckley's thugs would beat them up. As yet, the secret ballet had not been adopted in San Francisco. But the guards A. P. hired, in addition to the employees of his own business whom he sent out to protect voters, prevented large-scale intimidation. These tactics worked well for the reformers, who swept the election, not only in A. P.'s district, but throughout the city. Phelan emerged triumphant as the city's new mayor. And in the week following the election, A. P. scoured the North Beach neighborhood again. This time, mingling easily with working people and shopkeepers, he thanked them for their support, passed out candy and cigars, and made sure that he had made a lasting, favorable impression. That was his style, in politics as in business. As he recalled: "I passed out more cigars after the election than before. We kept contact between elections. We exhibited friendliness when we were seeking nothing. The result was when election time came around next time, we were remembered. When you sell people, keep them sold. That applies to politics as well as business." Some of his critics charged him with being an excessive egotist and a cynic. But A. P. was a pragmatist who kept his eye on major goals and orchestrated the details to achieve them.

The election did much to bolster A. P.'s status in the North Beach community. Through the campaign he now became widely known to thousands of residents in the area, including many outside the world of business. To many he projected an image of integrity and efficiency, of honesty and trust, of being a pillar of the community, especially to many Italian-Americans who were still very suspicious in their new and unfamiliar home. The figure that A. P. cut in the mayoralty campaign of 1899 was to stand him in good stead in later years when he embarked on his career as a local banker.

But A. P.'s restlessness continued even after his foray into politics. His work at Scatena and Company went well, but the thrill of achievement was fading. After considerable thought about the matter, he decided in 1901 to take an early retirement. His motivation was probably complex, because he never fully articulated the reasons for his decision. In the decade before 1901 he had been making extensive investments in real estate, and he did need more time for their management. Financially he was secure, with a fortune of about $300,000 and an ample annual income. In addition, the sale of his half interest in Scatena and Sons netted him another $100,000, a significant sum at the time. But A. P. was not solely interested in money. "I don't want to be rich," he declared. "No man actually owns a fortune; it owns him." At the same time, he moved the family from San Francisco to the old Donnelly mansion in Burlingame, and soon thereafter to San Mateo, where he remained for the rest of his life. When an interviewer asked him in 1947 about his decision to retire, A. P. responded, "I didn't have the money itch, having retired from the wholesale fruit and produce business at thirty-one, after a thorough training in it for twelve years up. When it became the top firm in the business west of Chicago, and having then, as I thought, enough money to get along the remainder of my days, I had no further incentive for then continuing in business after it had reached its goal of the top leadership, and everybody so recognized it."

In 1901 A. P. thus turned to a new challenge, that of being a real estate investor. His timing was propitious because San Francisco's population was then growing very rapidly. Land prices shot up especially sharply in exclusive suburban communities such as Burlingame and San Mateo. Although he was really well versed in many of the intricacies of real estate, characteristically A. P. was determined to learn the business from the ground up. Thus he rented desk space at one of the oldest San Francisco real estate firms, Madison and Burke, where he conducted many of his transactions and where expertise was always near. Soon the same qualities that had led to his success in the commission trade manifested themselves in real estate. His knowledge of property values was phenomenal, and his judgments usually sound and unerring. His grasp of a total situation was sure, and his sense of timing finely honed. To secure more capital he brought Pop Scatena into some of his transactions. The two of them could draw on an extensive network of acquaintances and clients, not only in North Beach, but throughout California. Within two years they built a phenomenonally successful real estate firm. Once again, the man and his environment were well matched as his particular talents found extraordinary scope in the rapidly expanding economy of California.

But just as A. P. was on his way to building a new real estate empire, unforeseen circumstances caused him to veer from his path. Somewhat unexpectedly, in June of 1902, his father-in-law, Joseph Cuneo, died at the age of ninety-one. Cuneo had become very fond of A. P. and had high respect for his business acumen. In fact, he named A. P as executor of his vast estate, which comprised more than one hundred separate parcels of property, totaling more than $500,000. Cuneo had eleven children, including grown sons, and the division of his properties was difficult, to say the least. With the consent of the widow, the family agreed to keep the real estate holdings intact and to appoint A. P. as their manager for a period of ten years. If he proved able to increase the capital value of the properties, he was to receive 25 percent of the increase. In view of the large and diverse nature of these real estate holdings, the task was not easy. But by 1911 A. P. had done well, earning $36,994 in fees, in addition to some shares of stock.

Upon A. P. now fell another of Cuneo's business activities, a directorship in a local bank. Cuneo had also been a director and principal stockholder of the Columbus Savings and Loan Society, a small bank catering almost exclusively to the Italian-American community of North Beach. When Cuneo died, the responsibility became A. P.'s. Initially the other directors welcomed him with open arms because of his extensive business experience and high standing among Italian-Americans in the neighborhood. At his insistence, they also appointed his father, Lorenzo Scatena, to the board. Although both men continued to devote most of their time to their respective business affairs, they now also turned their interests and their talents to the field of banking.

The Columbus Savings and Loan Society was the first bank to be established in the Italian-American community of North Beach. It was founded in 1893 by John F. Fugazi, one of the best-known Italian-Americans in San Francisco, and perhaps the West. His economic interests were as diverse as they were far-flung. Among his many ventures was his lucrative franchise for the White Star Line in San Francisco, an important shipping company. He also controlled its branches in other cities. As owner of one of the few large safes in North Beach, he stored the gold that many of his countrymen brought to him for safekeeping, or for remitting funds to their relatives in Europe. Somewhat gradually, therefore, Fugazi drifted into the banking business. Most Italians greatly mistrusted people outside their own ethnic community. Moreover, many had problems with English, so Fugazi concluded that it would be profitable for one of their countrymen to provide them with banking services. Although 1893 was a depression year, he established a small bank, the Columbus Savings and Loan Society, across the street from his travel agency, to serve their needs. His major adviser in the venture was Isaias W. Hellman, Sr., the influential president of the Nevada National Bank of San Francisco. Hellman, a German-Jewish immigrant, had started in Los Angeles thirty-six years earlier just like Fugazi—as a general store owner with a large safe who gradually drifted into banking.

During its first decade this little institution performed somewhat limited services for its Italian-American clients, almost all of them in the North Beach area. It provided a place of safekeeping for deposits, it extended construction loans for home builders, and it made limited loans to local businessman. Nevertheless, its policies were extremely conservative, reflecting the outlook of its directors and also of its clients, many of them former peasants. The directors tended to favor only people whom they knew well, who, if not fully established, were already prosperous. They had no inclination to promote entrepreneurs who were just starting or borrowers who desired small loans for short periods.

Meanwhile, in 1899 Andrea E. Sbarboro, another wealthy Italian-American in North Beach, founded a competing institution, the Italian-American Bank. Sbarboro had come to San Francisco from Italy in 1852 and made a fortune as a real estate developer. Over the years he lent liberally to thousands of small home builders in the San Francisco Bay area, in addition to founding the Italian-Swiss wine colony at Asti, California. More aggressive as a banker than Fugazi, his new bank offered a much wider range of services. Essentially a commercial institution, it provided its customers with checking accounts and was more liberal in its lending policies. By the time A. P. joined the board of directors of the Columbus Savings and Loan Society, the Italian-American Bank had become the leading financial institution in North Beach.

A. P. wanted to change all that. Given his competitive instincts, he found the situation appalling. He simply hated to be associated with a business that stood still. His vision was also closely tied to his expectations about California's future, a future that in his mind included the possibility of an almost limitless economic expansion. Moreover, he perceived what most other businessmen and bankers of his time still did not grasp, namely, that a huge mass market was growing in the West that as yet was still untapped. Until the early twentieth century, bankers had catered primarily to the upper classes in society. J. P. Morgan was a symbol of that generation, mainly serving the captains of industry. But A. P. recognized that in the twentieth century large profits could be made by catering to the masses—to the millions of people with modest means. It was this perception, combined with his many other talents, that was to make him the West's leading banker during the next few decades.

Not very long after he took his seat as a director of the Columbus Savings and Loan Society, A. P. suggested a wide range of changes to be made in its policies. He believed, for example, that the bank was not lending out a sufficient portion of its funds—that its loan practices were overly conservative. He felt strongly that it was operating far below its earning potential. On the basis of his own experience in real estate, A. P. was convinced that the bank had to make more loans based on landed properties.

THE NEXT TWO PAGES ARE IMPORTANT as THEY TELL WHAT MADE HIM START BANK OF ITA.

24   A. P. GIANNINI AND THE BANK OF AMERICA

In addition, A. P. criticized the special perquisites of the institution's officers. Usually, when borrowers came to the Columbus Savings bank for a loan, the officers forced them to carry fire insurance, which the officers themselves sold exclusively. As agents of insurance companies, they personally pocketed the commissions. A. P., however, was convinced that such proceeds should be paid to the bank, not to its employees.

He also argued that the bank should look beyond the Italian-American community to attract other ethnic groups. Such individuals, A. P. argued, constituted a fine market for small loans. North Beach was growing at the rate of two thousand people each year, and A. P. saw these newcomers as potential customers. True, most of them were poor, but he viewed them not as they were then but as what they might be in the future. His expectations were based on his own family's experience and that of thousands of other Italian-Americans whom he knew. Within a few years he expected many of them to be prosperous, and then they would be grateful clients of the institutions that had given them a start. Now was the time to win their loyalty. He knew that the officers of the large San Francisco banks, such as Crocker-Woolworth, looked upon most immigrants with disdain, particularly if they were not fluent in English. Since many of the immigrants only sought loans of less than $500, sums considered too puny by most established banks, the new migrants were forced to turn to loan sharks, who charged exorbitant fees.

Recalling his own experiences, A. P. was convinced that the bank should do much more to cultivate the patronage of small businessmen in North Beach. Existing policies of Columbus Savings simply did not provide for reaching out to such potential clients. But with his wide-ranging contacts in the Italian-American community, A. P. was convinced that he could attract hundreds, if not thousands, of new clients. After all, when he had been only fifteen years old, he had gone out successfully to recruit scores of new customers, and he was sure he could do it again.

In his analysis of Columbus Savings financial policies, A. P. had the full support of his father, but he ran into the bitter opposition of the other directors. After just a few meetings this conservative group of traditionalists seriously resented the newcomer in their midst. The more forceful he became, the icier was their response. "Go out and solicit . . . loans," A. P. told them at one meeting. "We should loan the bank's money right up to the hilt." That suggestion earned him the hostility of most of the directors, including that of Fugazi and his two sons on the board. And when Scatena went to Italy to visit relatives, his enemies on the board voted to oust him. A. P. was furious. "All right," he is reputed to have said. "I'll start a clean bank, run for the little fellow." He angrily stalked out and later sent them his resignation.

With his fighting instincts at a boiling point, A. P. now decided to establish his own bank. He felt that he knew little about finance, however. Thus he visited a close friend of his from commission trade days—James J. Fagan, who was a vice-president of American National Bank in San Francisco. Scatena and Company had kept its accounts there, and Fagan had handled many of its transactions. Reportedly A. P. burst into Fagan's office and shouted: "Giacomo, I'm going to start a bank. Tell me how to do it." Whether or not he used this exact language cannot be documented, but whatever he said, the episode represented the gist of his intentions.

And so, in 1904, A. P. made the fateful decision to devote all of his energies and talents to the banking business. It was a choice that was significant for himself, for California, and for the West. In retrospect, almost everything he had done in his life until then had prepared him for this new and greater challenge. The hard bargaining he had done in his rise as a commission merchant, his adroit real estate investments, and his brief involvement with local politics had honed his skills. No less important were the frustrations he experienced as a director of the Columbus Savings and Loan Association. The experience provided him with insights into the world of banking and an approach about how not to run a bank. In particular and distinctive ways, all of these stages in his life prepared him superbly for his future career. And the broader scale of the financial world was to suit his restless temperament far more than the more limited scope of the fruit commission business.

A. P. now turned the same characteristics that had stood him in good stead to banking. His psychological insights into human nature were considerable. His entrepreneurial abilities were as diverse as they were uncanny. His managerial and organizational skills matched his imagination and vision. In his recognition of the potentials of a mass market rather than those of a class market, he was at least a generation ahead of most others. His abilities to manipulate politics to his own advantage were striking. His sense of judgment was usually sound and accurate. His timing was as sensitive as it was precise. His ability to anticipate and to adapt new business methods was superior to most of his contemporaries in the field. Added to these qualities was a boundless capacity for hard work; in fact, working around the clock was his major preoccupation and joy. In addition, he had a well-developed competitive spirit, aggressiveness, and forcefulness that sometimes degenerated into ruthlessness and dictatorial tendencies. All of these qualities were to be reflected in his banking practices, for in many ways the bank he was about to build was an extension of his personality.

Without doubt, much of A. P.'s success was due to such personal characteristics, but he was also fortunate in operating in an environment that provided considerable scope for a man like himself. California was in the throes of rapid growth during the first decades of the twentieth century and provided ample opportunities for entrepreneurial experimentation. It encouraged many other men who were dreamers and builders and who wedded their own fulfillment to the economic development of the state and the West. These men included Arthur Mulholland, builder of the Los Angeles Aqueduct; Henry J. Kaiser, maker of roads and dams; Henry B. Mayer, the Hollywood tycoon; and others like them, all of whom A. P. knew. They were individuals of gargantuan ambitions who found a panorama in California that was unmatched elsewhere in the United States. It was in this atmosphere of frenzied growth, of unprecedented ambitions, that A. P. found his métier. He not only would become the builder of a new bank—the best and largest in the state—but he would contribute significantly to the growth of his beloved native state and of the West. In the process he genuinely hoped to improve the welfare and the lives of thousands of individuals, the little people, including the sons and daughters of immigrants like himself. Perhaps they too could partake of the American Dream as he himself and his family had done. A later generation of historians, bred and nurtured in affluence, might scoff at the suppositions of men like A. P. But to him and his contemporaries, such goals seemed as real as they were genuine. These were challenges that stimulated the imagination. In 1904 A. P. thus turned his prodigious talents to the attainment of his new and broader goals.

CHAPTER 2

Building an Empire, 1905–1919

THE opening years of the century coincided with another era of prosperity for California and much of the West. The nation finally emerged from the severe depression of the 1890s. Population soared as unprecedented numbers of foreign immigrants poured into cities east and west. Although a majority of the one million or so newcomers who came each year between 1900 and 1910 settled in the ethnic neighborhoods of large eastern cities like Boston and New York, substantial numbers also came to West Coast urban areas, boosting their already high rate of population growth. The seventeen states west of the Mississippi River grew from 6.3 million in 1900 to 17.9 million twenty years later. In such an economic environment an imaginative entrepreneur like A. P. perceived extraordinary opportunities. Moreover, by this time many bankers and businessmen agreed that the existing banking structure of the United States was too inflexible and archaic to meet the needs of a rapidly expanding economy. Such a recognition led President Theodore Roosevelt to appoint the National Banking Commission in 1907 to study bank practices in the United States and around the world. Its task was to recommend new policies for American banks in a rapidly changing economic situation. Perceptive individuals like A. P. were sensitive to these trends while at the same time reveling in the dynamic business environment that he saw all about him. It was a time for action and change, not for standing still.

Such conditions were ideally suited to A. P.'s restless personality. To challenge seemingly stodgy banking practices such as he had found at the Columbus Savings and Loan Association whetted his competitive instincts. Here were the new challenges he had been seeking. Not only would he question the viability of the old ways of banking, he would provide leadership for the new, for the creation of new forms of banking, for trying out novel techniques on the basis of his experiences in his several successful business ventures. In

27

particular, he was concerned with the development of a mass market, a venture still ignored by most other bankers. Moreover, his style in combining the drive for profit with service to his clients, accompanied with a human touch, had a distinctive flair. The prospect of developing a network of tens of thousands—perhaps even hundreds of thousands—of satisfied customers who looked to him for a variety of essential services appealed enormously to his ego. Mere monetary profit alone could not provide him with such personal fulfillment and sense of power. As the commission business and real estate had done, so his new bank would become a vehicle for satisfying many of his emotional needs and would provide him with the challenge he had been seeking.

Soon after his visit to James J. Fagan, A. P. began in earnest to make plans for his new bank. Using his well-honed powers of persuasion, he talked five former directors of the Columbus Savings and Loan Association into joining the board of his fledgling institution. In addition, he persuaded four friends from his produce and realty days to become directors. Fagan, his old banker, also agreed to take a seat on the board, the only Irish-American in a group otherwise entirely of Italian origins. The directors represented a wide range of business experience. Antonio Chichizola, for example, was an importer, Giacome Costa a real estate investor, and Luigi de Martini a confectioner. During May and June of 1904 the group met daily with A. P. and his father, Lorenzo Scatena, discussing plans and prospective policies. A. P. was elated, bubbling with enthusiasm, full of ideas and projects. On August 10, 1904, he secured the necessary legal papers for incorporation of the new Bank of Italy with a capital of $300,000. It was designed to be both a savings as well as a commercial bank. In selecting the premises for the institution, A. P. leased the Drexler Building, a three-story structure at the intersection of Columbus Avenue and Washington Street in San Francisco. To add insult to injury, the directors of the Columbus Savings and Loan Association suddenly found that A. P. was their new landlord and that he was opening a competing bank on the same site as theirs. They resorted to legal action in an attempt to oust him but were unsuccessful. One did not trifle with A. P.! Apart from his sense of glee at their predicament, he liked the location because it was just one block away from the city jail. A. P. reasoned that this would afford him excellent police protection, since officers came and went night and day.

On October 17, 1904, A. P. opened the fledgling Bank of Italy for business. From the very start A. P. did what he had always done in his previous ventures—he went out to the streets to hustle and to solicit new accounts. On the first day he went to visit many of his old customers in the fruit and vegetable trade, persuading many to make transactions at his fledgling bank. Aware of the vast untapped market in rural areas like the Sacramento Valley, he went there as well, offering loans to farmers. In addition, he broke existing traditions in the banking business by widespread advertising of his just-established institution. Other bankers were scandalized because advertising was a practice that most financiers of that day simply eschewed. Many considered even the solicitation of accounts to be uncouth and unprofessional, if not downright unethical. But A. P. believed in setting precedents. And he delighted in the value of shock appeal. "How can people know what a bank can and will do for them unless they're told?" he asked. "I'm going to tell everybody about this bank and what we're going to try to do here in any way I can, by word of mouth, newspaper, or any other medium I can think of." Within a month he had garnered a respectable number of commission house accounts from North Beach, and also individual accounts from Italian-Americans in the area. By December 1904 his bank had $285,000 in resources and $109,000 in deposits. At that point A. P. decided that he should pay a 5 percent dividend to his stockholders to enhance his favorable image. Throughout his career, he believed in the payment of dividends whenever possible as a means of retaining a loyal following.

A. P. also decided to attract customers whom other bankers spurned. His campaigns brought people to his door who had never used a bank before, or who in many instances could not speak or write English. The bank's three employees helped them to fill out forms and deposit slips. Many of these individuals were workingmen, small trades types, fish dealers, grocers, draymen, bakers, plumbers, and barbers, all of whom A. P. educated in the use of banks.

A. P.'s knowledge of human nature was also reflected in the selection of his initial staff of three. He hired an assistant cashier, a teller, and a stenographer. As cashier A. P. chose Armando Pedrini, a handsome Italian immigrant who had worked for the Columbus Savings and Loan Society. To wean him away A. P. had to double his salary. When his dubious directors questioned him about the wisdom of such seeming extravagance and pressed him to explain why he would go to such lengths, A. P. responded: "Because he knows his business. The women are crazy about him [he would kiss their hands in Continental style], and he gives a man in overalls as much attention as a big depositor."

During his first year A. P. steered his bank into promoting real estate development in North Beach. Most of the loans he approved were for builders or commission merchants who were seeking to expand their operations. But A. P. also pioneered in making personal loans as small as $25, something other bankers did not do. By encouraging small accounts and loans, the bank was tapping funds that otherwise had not been placed in banks. Many Italians preferred to keep their money under mattresses and in assorted hiding places in their homes or back yards. As A. P. surmised correctly, some of the poor immigrants of 1904 were bound to be affluent citizens two decades later. His policy was to build a tradition of good will. He wanted their gratitude and loyalty as well as their business. His insight was sound. After about ten months he found that he needed to enlarge his premises.

Throughout 1905 and the first quarter of 1906, the bank continued on the path of slow and steady growth. But then an unforeseen event provided it with an unexpected boost. That event was the San Francisco earthquake, which shook unwary citizens at 5:00 A.M. on the morning of April 18, 1906. The tremors themselves lasted only twenty-eight seconds, but the devastation emanating from them persisted for years. Upon feeling the first shocks, scores of San Franciscans ran into the streets. Many of these thoroughfares had suffered structural damage, and water and gas lines broke in profusion. Still, in the first few hours after the initial shocks, it appeared that most buildings in the business district had withstood the shock. The situation was worse in the southern part of the city, between Market Street and the bay, where the quake leveled hundreds of more flimsy structures. As the day progressed, however, the situation worsened. After the collapse of houses and the bursting of gas pipes and water mains came the fires, rampaging in many neighborhoods. Increasingly the fire department had to watch helplessly as the inferno spread because there was no water in the mains.

A. P. was not in the city when the quake first struck. But he did feel the tremors in his San Mateo home. Anxious to discover the exact nature of the disaster, he dressed quickly, gulped down a hasty breakfast, and hurried to the commuter rail station, where he usually boarded a train to travel to the city. A noisy crowd had gathered there, and he listened to excited people discussing all kinds of rumors. No one had precise information about the rapidly changing situation. After some waiting, at last a train pulled in, and A. P. boarded it with the restless throng. But the train crept along with agonizing slowness, obviously unable to keep to its regular schedule. What usually took thirty minutes now took three hundred! Nor was the train able to reach its regular downtown destination. Instead, it stopped on the outskirts of the city at the old 22d Street and Valencia station. That was the end of the line for this particular day, a conductor's voice boomed over the loudspeaker. A. P. now wasted little time. He ran into the streets, determined to walk the rest of the way to look at the condition of his beloved bank.

Meanwhile, initial calm prevailed at the Bank of Italy. At about 9:00 A.M. Pedrini opened the premises, relieved that the bank building had sustained only minor damage. As yet, he had not heard any news of spreading fires. Not much transpired until noon, when A. P. finally arrived, five hours after he had left San Mateo, about seventeen miles to the south. He quickly surveyed the situation and concluded (quite accurately, as later events would prove) that fires would spread to the business district within a few hours and destroy his bank. His sharp eyes had also discerned looters already on the prowl.

In view of these circumstances A. P. decided to close the institution early and to move its assets and its books to his home in San Mateo. The problem was how to navigate through clogged streets and roads and how to protect his gold and cash in this chaotic atmosphere. A. P. pondered the unusual situation quickly and then rushed into action. He contacted his father, Pop Scatena, who was in his commission business office, and requested two teams of horses, two wagons, and about a dozen crates of fruits and vegetables. By 5:00 P.M. the two wagons were in front of A. P.'s bank. Then he and his staff loaded the bank's available cash and about $80,000 in gold on the wagon beds and piled the bank's records and produce crates on top.

Meanwhile, chaos in the city was spreading. Thousands of people milled about in the streets with their belongings. Some were in confusion, and others hoped to escape to the safety of the outer suburbs. Still keeping an eye out for would-be robbers, A. P. decided to wait until dark before attempting to start out for San Mateo. Yet he could hardly tarry near his bank, since he expected it to be engulfed by fire within a few hours, or perhaps even within minutes. Thus he

resolved to park the wagons at the apartment of Clarence Cuneo, his
brother-in-law, who lived near Francisco and Jones streets at the far
end of the North Beach area. As yet, that section had been spared
from fire. At Cuneo's place he ate a quick supper and also secured a
few mattresses to pile on the wagons for additional camouflage. By
about 8:00 P.M. darkness rolled in, and the two wagons—drawn by
A. P.'s favorite and faithful mares—embarked on the trip to A. P.'s
home in San Mateo. A. P. and Pedrini steered one of the vehicles,
while Cuneo and A. P.'s brother directed the other.

The journey proved to be difficult and tedious. Roads were clogged
with thousands of panic-stricken refugees from the city. Everywhere
debris was strewn across streets and thoroughfares. Many places were
flooded because of broken water mains. Here and there the way was
blocked, and everywhere they could see the red hue of the sky from
the fires in the city. It made the entire spectacle dramatic, if somewhat
macabre. The trip, which usually took three hours by wagon, lasted
the entire night. When they finally arrived at A. P.'s home in the early
morning hours, A. P. quickly stashed his bank's money in the ash
trap of his fireplace in the living room. Although exhausted, he was
elated that he had completed the journey without mishap. "I was
never so relieved in my life as when I pulled up in front of the house,"
he said. "We didn't have any guards. All the police and soldiers were
busy fighting the fire. It was extremely difficult to disguise the load
we were carrying, and I thought I saw would-be robbers on every
street corner. The idea of the crates worked, but for weeks after the
earthquake the bank's money smelled like orange juice." Even after
he stashed the gold away, he was still uneasy. Thus, he sent Pedrini
and Cuneo to the first floor of his house to watch the driveway, while
he and his brother guarded the fireplace. "None of us got much
sleep," A. P. later remembered—"one or two hours, but I wouldn't
risk leaving the fireplace. We were all grateful when the hours went
by and nothing happened."

Although extremely tired, A. P. could not rest. He had been awake
for more than twenty-four hours, but his thoughts were of the burn-
ing inferno he had left. What was the fate of his bank? Was the
building still standing? On Thursday of that week he tried to rest as
best he could. But on Friday, April 20, 1906, he decided to return to
San Francisco to survey the situation for himself. What he saw was
disheartening. The fire had transformed most of the financial district,
including the building housing the Bank of Italy, into ashes and

rubble. Even the bank's safe had become a lump of molten iron. By then one-third of the city had been laid to waste, including more than five hundred city blocks containing twenty-eight thousand buildings. At least 500 people had lost their lives, and 250,000 were homeless. Estimates of property losses ranged upward of $500 million.

Amid such desolation, the spirits of many people simply flagged. Bewilderment, fear, uncertainty, and insecurity gripped hundreds of thousands of San Franciscans, refugees as well as those who were fortunate enough to have escaped much of the destruction. No one sized up the psychological mood more quickly than A. P., always quick to note human frailties and strengths. The most valuable resource of a bank, he surmised, was not really its cash reserve but rather the degree to which it provided its customers with a sense of security. That was a psychological rather than a strictly economic commodity. Clearly, cash reserves were a means to the achievement of that end, but not an end in themselves.

With his intuitive grasp of the big picture, A. P. decided to wrest opportunity from disaster. At 1:00 P.M. on Saturday, April 21, 1906, he attended a meeting of businessmen near the waterfront, who had gathered to discuss the current situation. Representatives of the great banks in San Francisco who were there declared that they most likely would not be able to reopen their institutions until November. It might take weeks to open their vaults because of the intense heat that had been generated in them by the fire. No one would know for quite a while, therefore, what had been saved and what had been destroyed. But A. P. strenuously disagreed with their assessment. "Gentlemen," he is reported to have said, "to follow the course you are suggesting will be a vital mistake. . . . We've got to fight our way out of this spot. If you keep your banks closed until November . . . there will be no city or people left to serve. Today is the time they need you. The time for doing business is right now. Tomorrow morning I am putting a desk on Washington Street wharf with a Bank of Italy sign over it. Any man who wants to rebuild San Francisco can come there and get as much cash as he needs to do it." And he stomped out of the meeting to make the necessary preparations for his next day's operations.

That night he returned home to finalize his plans. And on the next day, as the fires began to burn themselves out, he brought $10,000 in cash from his San Mateo hoard to the desk on the wharf with a sign announcing that he was once again open for business. At the same time, he placed advertisements in local newspapers to publicize the resumption of his normal banking services. He spread word of its activities everywhere, but particularly among the Italians in the North Beach neighborhood. As he proudly declared in an advertisement in the *San Francisco Chronicle,* the city's major newspaper, "Bank of Italy now open for regular business." Always a showman, he made sure that his desk on the wharf was picturesque and striking. He installed a plank counter in front of his desk, the plank resting on one barrel at each end. On top of that he placed a big sack of gold. A cardboard sign proclaimed that the Bank of Italy functioned there, that it was open, and that it was ready for business. P. T. Barnum could hardly have done better.

At the same time, A. P. sought to reassure his nervous depositors. On Sunday, April 22, he sent them a circular letter announcing that his bank would open temporary offices in the undamaged home of his brother, Dr. Attilio Giannini, at 2745 Van Ness Avenue as well as on the wharf at the foot of Washington Street. The bank would cash checks and would also consider loans for reconstruction projects. Meanwhile, other banks took much longer to start up their operations. They had few options but to wait at least one month or more before their vaults had cooled enough to allow them to open the doors so as to secure access to their funds. But in the month following the earthquake, the Bank of Italy was fully operative. Each day A. P. would bring a bag of gold from his house in San Mateo to provide cash for loans. One San Franciscan recalled that A. P. stood on the wharf, consoling his Italian compatriots, "We're going to rebuild San Francisco, and it will be better than ever. . . ." This observer noted that "all of us kept out of his way in those days. He was too busy to do anything except take care of customers."

Moreover, just as he had advised farmers on business practices during his commission firm days, so now A. P. provided advice for many who were involved in the arduous task of reconstruction. Most bankers in the city were waiting for insurance companies to compensate homeowners before resuming loans. But not A. P. He decided to accelerate the process. Contacting a number of ship captains who operated small vessels in the bay and whom he had known in his days as a commission merchant, he lent them cash with which to purchase lumber in Washington and Oregon. "Get all the lumber you can," he said. "It will soon be in greater demand than anything else." Those who followed his advice made good profits and easily paid off the loans A. P. had extended. It was good business for him— and for them. As one of his associates noted: "With his experience and ability to see ahead, he could have made a fortune for himself out of the disaster. Instead, he passed the idea along to others." A. P. was not being altruistic. He was more concerned with a long-range policy of maintaining grateful customers over an extensive span of years than with making a quick killing.

The San Francisco earthquake, more than anything else during these years, made A. P. a local hero. It earned him a reputation for personal courage in rescuing the bank's money in the midst of fire and disaster. With his flair for showmanship, A. P. carefully nurtured and capitalized on this image. His decision to help earthquake victims to rebuild their homes—when other bankers were stalling—also set him apart from contemporaries in the field. Italian newspapers in the city such as *L'Italia* were unrestrained in their praise and their pride. Its editorial writers designated him as one of North Beach's "most progressive businessmen," as one who had brought "hope and confidence to so many people who had lost their homes in the fire." But the major newspapers now also took note of this new banker, this son of immigrants. The *San Francisco Call* went out of its way to commend his confidence in the "good faith and honesty of the homeless people of North Beach." His feats became one of the inspiring legends that were told about the great disaster.

Within a month A. P. was also busily at work to undertake the physical rebuilding of his bank. After some scurrying he found a sound building just across the street from his old quarters. The structure had been saved because it was near the U.S. Post Office, which federal troops had protected. By June 1906, while many of his competitors were still immobile, A. P.'s institution was busy and thriving. Every day he would personally authorize a large volume of loans, often on the basis of nothing more than his judgment. He lent gladly on real estate and on assets of small businesses. During the summer of 1906 he could look back on the doubling of his bank's transactions and deposits since its inception. Reflecting his confidence in the future of San Francisco, he now selected a new site for the bank on land he owned at Clay and Montgomery streets, two blocks closer to the financial district. There he planned to erect a nine-story building and to inaugurate another chapter in his institution's rapid development.

The San Francisco earthquake had a dramatic impact on A. P. and the Bank of Italy. It confirmed him in his decision to embark on a career as a banker. And it did much to accelerate the growth of the fledgling bank. A. P.'s dramatic gesture in reopening his bank just a few days after the disaster while most other financial institutions were closed created an image that set him apart from the rest. A. P. was always very conscious of images and their significance in the world of business. It also placed the public spotlight on what had been a small and obscure bank and attracted attention from other bankers and the general public. No advertising campaign could have accomplished what the earthquake did for him. And the experience confirmed A. P. in his views on what he considered to be efficient, sound, and forward-looking policies in the field of banking.

Now that he had decided to devote himself full time to the banking business, A. P. resolved to learn more about it. In March of 1907, therefore, he embarked on a combination vacation and business trip to New York City to survey the policies of the big eastern institutions and to meet their officers. He also visited Chicago and Philadelphia and on his return stopped in New Orleans. He found considerable pessimism among most bankers. As he reminisced in 1947: "I didn't say much, but I could see that they were depressed and down in the mouth." The currency was far too inelastic in the face of a rapidly expanding economy. And many banks were concerned about the decentralization of reserves they had on deposit. Smaller banks usually deposited such funds with large institutions in cities. But when at any one time a large number of the little banks demanded their reserve deposits, they placed great strains on their big-city cousins. This was especially true in 1907, when the San Francisco earthquake required huge payments by insurance companies. These totaled more than $200 million. Since most of the insurance firms were headquartered in the East, they made substantial withdrawals from big-city financial institutions, draining their reserves. The physical disaster in the West therefore had significant economic repercussions in the East.

As he surveyed the financial climate on his return to San Francisco in May of 1907, A. P. concluded that caution and prudence were now as essential in the current state of affairs as the solicitation of new business. He decided that his bank should increase its gold holdings, cut down on loans, and also seek to increase deposits. To accumulate gold he ordered his tellers to make payments with paper money whenever possible. He himself passed on every loan application that was submitted and raised his interest rates from 6 to 7 percent. Meanwhile, he again took to the streets to attract new deposits. By now he looked beyond the Italian community and was seeking a more diversified ethnic clientele. With that end in view he opened his first branch on August 1, 1907. It was located on Mission Street, in a neighborhood where there were few Italians. In contrast to most other bankers, his main aim was to cater to working people. Consequently he did not keep "banker's hours." Instead of expecting customers to conform to the hours set by bank officers, he attempted to adapt to the schedules of his clients. His branch was open in the evenings and even on Sundays—innovations scorned by his competitors.

A. P. also turned the financial panic of 1907 to his advantage. In October of 1907 a nationwide bank panic swept the nation, which also affected western institutions. Many small institutions in the region found that they were unable to call in their reserves deposited in hard-pressed big-city banks. Large and small were caught in a financial crunch, caused in part by the inflexibility of the existing national bank system. The governors of Nevada, Washington, and Oregon felt constrained to proclaim bank holidays to avert widespread bank failures in their respective states. On October 30, 1907, the crisis reached San Francisco. California's governor, James G. Gillette, also declared a bank holiday, to be in effect until December 21, although many banks continued to be open. The main purpose of this action was to help taxpayers, who under existing California law were required to make tax payments in gold. This bank crisis lasted about fifty days. Many large banks had to suspend gold payments because of specie shortages. But the Bank of Italy was able to continue its gold payments and to honor all its commitments because A. P. had had the foresight to accumulate ample reserves. Despite some difficulties, he ended the year with substantial increases in his bank's assets and its deposits. His performance during the panic further strengthened the image of the bank as an exceptionally well-managed and sound institution.

Since it was A. P.'s nature to be competitive, he was constantly searching for innovative methods. As in his earlier business dealings, he cultivated a wide network of friends and acquaintances in his field, and he was sensitive to nuances in the business climate. In May of 1908 he journeyed to Pasadena to attend the annual meeting of the California Bankers Association. There the major topic of discussion was, as might be imagined, the recent financial panic. Many of the speakers discussed ways and means of avoiding such stresses in the future. One of the presenters was Lyman J. Gage, who had been President William McKinley's secretary of the treasury. Gage had been greatly impressed by Canada's experience with branch banking, which, he believed, would avoid the kind of financial panics to which the United States seemed prone. A. P. was impressed by the proposal.

A few months later A. P. went to attend the annual convention of the American Bankers Association in Denver. Here the featured keynoter was Woodrow Wilson, then the president of Princeton University. In a speech that was not at all well received, Wilson, too, advocated branch banking as a means of preventing banking crises. As the future president noted:

> The banks of this country are remote from the people and the people regard them as not belonging to them but as belonging to some power hostile to them.
>
> If a system of branch banks very simply and inexpensively managed . . . could be established which would put the resources of the rich banks of the country at the disposal of whole countrysides to whose merchants and farmers only a restricted and local credit is now open, the attitude of plain men everywhere towards the banks and banking would be changed utterly within less than a generation. . . . There would be plenty of investments if you carried your investments to the people of the country at large and had agents in hundreds of villages who knew the men in their neighborhoods who could be trusted with loans and who would make profitable use of them. Your money, moreover, would quicken and fertilize the country.

Most of his listeners remained unimpressed, but not A. P. This suggestion by Wilson strengthened a train of thought that A. P. had been turning over in his mind for some months. Earlier that year he had taken a trip through western Canada, where he observed the operation of branch banking and came away deeply impressed. In remote communities like Medicine Hat he visited branches of Toronto and Montreal banks that performed services no independent small-town bank could have undertaken. Such institutions contrasted sharply with speculative wildcat banks often found in American frontier areas. A. P. rarely read history, for he was, above all, a practical man. But his firsthand inspection of the Canadian banking system, rather than any reading about it, convinced him that branch banking could be as successful in the United States as it had been in Canada for over half a century.

By 1908, therefore, A. P. was largely convinced that branch banking would provide California and the West with a flexible and sound banking system. At the same time, of course, it would serve as a prime means for the expansion of his own institution. Moreover, it meshed well with his own past experiences in relating the activities of a city bank to the special needs of the underdeveloped countryside. Branch banking seemed particularly suitable for newly settled areas such as California and the trans-Mississippi West. And it also suited his own temperament and his gargantuan ambitions in wanting to build the region's—and perhaps the nation's—largest bank. As he noted in 1927: "The development of our nation's resources demands big capital and large institutions to handle it in mobile form like the direction of an army in the field, so that forces can be shifted from place to place where most needed. The small banks, even in interior towns, can no longer meet the requirements of intricate and far-reaching business demands. Interests of large territorial spread can no longer depend upon smaller banks to finance them and carry their accounts from town to town." And as he crystallized his ideas in later years, he said succinctly (in 1943) that branch banking was "the only way that a small town can get the resources, [the] brain power, and equipment of a billion dollar bank. And when they've got it, the town starts growing."

His enthusiasm was such that when in 1908 and 1909 the California legislature enacted a comprehensive new state banking law, it reflected his advocacy of branch banking. The California Bankers Association at its 1908 Pasadena meeting had appointed a committee to draft the major provisions of a comprehensive new state banking act. The lawmakers accepted most of the recommendations of this group, including one innocuous clause providing for branch banking, which hitherto had been neither allowed nor forbidden. The Banking Act of 1909 contained the as yet uncontroversial provision to permit branch banking in California, provided that the newly created office of state superintendent of banking approved all applications for such branches.

Meanwhile, A. P. busied himself with the expansion of his bank. On August 17, 1908, he proudly moved into his new nine-story building, which symbolized a giant step forward for his fledgling institution. A reporter for the *Coast Banker* glowingly described the new edifice and the image it projected:

> The building is noteworthy, because of its beauty and completeness and because it illustrates the enterprise of the management on account of the fact that it was one of the first big structures to be erected after

the fire. The structure is all of steel and is absolutely fireproof. . . . The building is of most enduring construction. . . . Free rein has been given to artists and architects to carry out the general idea of the management to make the banking room ideally beautiful. . . . No banking room in this city will excel [it] in beauty. . . . Pavanazzo marble walls, desks, railings, partitions, counters and vault fronts, Italian marble flooring, bronze doors, window frames and candelabras and counter screens together with a most elaborate ceiling of complex lines heavily laid in gold and high color, and set off by richly wrought electroliers from wall surfaces and bronze stands, constitute the items of finish that go to make up a perfect composition.

Meanwhile, A. P. was developing strategies to stimulate his bank's growth. One dramatic gesture that he made in his new building was to refuse to sit in a closed office. Most bank presidents of his day were inaccessible to the public, one convention that A. P. reveled in openly bucking. He seated himself at a large desk in an open area on the first floor of the bank, where he was available to one and all. He enjoyed the human contact that this exposure provided him and at the same time exuded an atmosphere of openness that made his bank distinctive. It was a practice to which he held most of his life, even after he was head of a billion-dollar institution.

More than other bankers, A. P. relied on advertising and publicity to recruit customers. Others at this time frowned on the practice. In the World War I era he still tended to place a special emphasis on neighborhoods or small towns with a large number of Italians. True, Italian-Americans were not numerous enough to be a powerful political or economic pressure group on a statewide basis. But they were important in particular industries, such as the wineries, or in selected regions, such as the San Joaquin Valley. In such communities he would conduct personal public relations campaigns, going from door to door, shaking hands with store owners as well as people on the street. During these veritable blitzes he would pass out hundreds of handbills designed to educate people in the use of banks. "It is never easy to save money," one of these announced, "but when you do, place it in a safe bank instead of hiding it in a mattress where thieves can steal it, or fire can destroy it." Another advised that "in order to purchase your home, put aside a certain amount each week or each month." These campaigns usually netted him a significant number of new depositors. Many of them would become lifelong clients who utilized the increasingly diversified services of A. P.'s institution.

He also persuaded some of these people to become stockholders, tying them more closely to the bank. Under ordinary circumstances he did not sell large blocks of stocks to outsiders, lest it interfere with his absolute, and usually autocratic, control of the bank. Instead, he preferred to sell five to ten shares per person, which enabled him to raise considerable cash from large numbers of people without giving them an influential voice in the institution's policies.

Once A. P. had established a beachhead with a new branch, he would move in with his campaign staff to inundate the area and win new accounts. Eventually he would reach out to minorities in California other than Italians—mainly Yugoslavs, Russians, Greeks, Mexicans, and Portuguese—developing advertising materials in their respective languages and hiring multilingual bank staff. Once his branch had gained a measure of stability and respectability, he would seek to expand his reach further by appealing to the non-foreign-born population. He used this formula again and again in coming years as branch banking became his major strategy for growth. "By opening branches, I saw that we could give better service to everybody," A. P. declared in later years. "There would be no need for anyone to make a long trip, say from a distant part of the state into San Francisco, for all the credit he might require. Each branch would be a business-getter for the institution as a whole, but each branch likewise would have behind it the resources the bank possessed. We would be able to care for the needs of any customer." That, in a nutshell, was the rationale behind the campaign for branch banking that he began in 1909 soon after he opened his first branch in San Francisco.

As he studied the Bank Act of 1909, A. P. became convinced that it meant to encourage the growth of branch banking. Actually, this was a nonissue in 1909. The lawmakers had included such a provision in Section 9 largely to give the superintendent of banking broad powers. He alone in the state had authority to grant permission to any bank applying for the opening of new branches. But given his newly found fascination with branch banking, A. P. read this obscure clause as an official encouragement to open new outlets. Soon after passage of the law he secured approval of his board of directors to open a branch outside San Francisco.

Quite naturally, A.P.'s thoughts turned first to his hometown of San Jose. The Santa Clara Valley seemed ripe for further development. Since he had grown up there many thousands of new immigrants had poured in, often settling on small farms. Remembering his own family's experiences, A. P. believed that many of them could prosper more if they had access to additional capital and credit. He also knew that quite a few spoke no English and were unfamiliar with American business methods. Established bankers just ignored or even shunned them. In any case, small borrowers almost always had to pay much higher rates of interest than did large landowners. A. P. hoped to change this situation. Obviously, he was not a philanthropist, but he saw unexploited opportunities for his bank in an as yet uncultivated market, opportunities that traditional bankers simply ignored.

Thus he began in 1909 to plan for a new branch in San Jose. Here, as in the future, he usually preferred to acquire an existing institution rather than to start from scratch. When he attended a Columbus Day celebration there, he used the occasion to sound out leaders of the Italian-American community about the possibility of a branch there. Generally, they were encouraging and referred him to Lazard Lion, president of the oldest and largest bank in the city. This was the Commercial and Savings Bank, at the time suffering under a high burden of debt because of poor management. A. P. was eager to acquire such a staid, and formerly prestigious, institution and instructed his able legal counsel, James Bacigalupi, to work out details of a purchase. As they were able to do in many such deals in the future, the Giannini team drove a hard bargain but came out successfully. Bacigalupi also secured approval by the state superintendent of banks. Within a month a proud A. P. opened the doors to his new branch. As his advertisement in the *San Jose Mercury and Herald* of November 14, 1909 noted:

> The new institution is to pay special attention to the affairs of people who speak English with difficulty and will have employees who speak the French, Italian, Spanish and Portuguese languages.
> "The transformation of the local bank into a branch of the San Francisco institution," stated Dr. A. H. Giannini [brother of A. P.] "does not mean that San Jose coin will be taken away to San Francisco, but that San Francisco coin will be brought into San Jose. The officers are in no way intruders in the local field as many of them are very well known in the community, having lived here."

A. P. made a special appeal to ethnic minorities. In what was to become a familiar technique in his acquisitions policies, he appointed representatives of the immigrant communities in San Jose to various jobs in the bank and to a newly created advisory board. All employees of the bank were required to speak Italian and at least one other foreign language. To his advisory board he appointed mostly Italians, such as Attilio Giannini, N. A. Pellerano, E. A. Filipello, and others like L. V. Slavich and Jesse Levy. A. P. also made sure that representatives of old, established families in the area, often WASPs, would be represented. With such methods he was able to increase substantially the San Jose branch's business within the first year of operation.

As in future years, A. P. confounded fellow bankers by his novel policies. He deliberately sought out "little people," rather than those of means. "The 'little fellow' is the best customer that a bank can have," A. P. said. "He starts with you and stays to the end; whereas the big fellow is only with you so long as he can get something out of you, and when he cannot, he is not for you any more." He kept his San Jose branch open during evening hours and on Saturdays so that local farmers could use his banking services at convenient times. And to entice them further, he offered them loans two to five percentage points cheaper than charged by the competition. To win the support of old customers at the bank who had been with the predecessor institution, he promised to reduce interest rates on their outstanding loans, so that they too would pay no more than the current 7 percent interest that he charged. "You are putting borrowers out of business if you charge 10 or 12 per cent," he said. "The man who will fight for cheaper interest rates is the one we want to loan money to."

Success in San Jose whetted A. P.'s desire to extend his branch system. By 1910 he was beginning to build a network of contacts in the banking profession that provided information on the condition of banks in California, especially those that might be ripe for sale. His trusted adviser James J. Fagan, now with Crocker National Bank, served on his board of directors and was a key figure on potential acquisitions. Through Fagan and his friends A. P. learned of two weak banks in San Francisco that he might easily purchase. One was the Citizen's National Bank, and the other was the Mechanics' Savings Bank. A. P. began to watch them like a hawk and within a year had worked out the complicated negotiations that brought them under his control. His fertile imagination now developed additional techniques to drum up business. He hired salesmen to go from door to door in San Francisco's Italian community to explain the advantages of opening a savings account at the Bank of Italy. His sales force rarely slept, and he drove them mercilessly. They attended weddings, baptisms, community picnics, church services, and all kinds of social occasions. No other bankers used such tactics. Within two years these high-pressure methods resulted in a doubling of the number of accounts at his San Francisco institutions.

But A. P. was already dreaming big dreams and looking beyond California. In July 1912 he opened his second branch outside San Francisco, in San Mateo. Meanwhile, he went on a business trip to New York City in November 1911, where he became involved in negotiations to buy a small New York City bank located in Brooklyn. His eyes were on the almost one million Italian immigrants in the New York area, who offered a large potential market. The Italian-American businessmen there were amenable but wanted him to devote his managerial talents full-time to the New York venture. At this stage in his career A. P. was unwilling to leave California, and the deliberations collapsed. But they revealed that while he was still a relatively small, obscure California banker, his ambitions already extended beyond California, to the West, and indeed to the entire nation.

Although A. P. concluded in 1912 that the time was not ripe for extending to New York, he found the prospects for expansion into southern California were positively exciting. Between 1900 and 1910 the population of Los Angeles tripled—from 102,000 to 319,000, — while the state's general population grew at a slower rate. In contrast, San Francisco's growth had slowed to a rate of about 20 percent increase in the century's first decade. The boosters of Los Angeles, like William Mulholland, were making grandiose plans for a future metropolis that would be the largest in the state as they built the Owens River Aqueduct, designed to provide for many millions. Los Angeles authorities were also expanding San Pedro harbor in their hope to challenge San Francisco's primacy as the Pacific Coast's leading port. And in the small suburb of Hollywood, a new film industry was taking root and, already by 1915, promised to become a major economic asset for southern California.

A. P. also perceived other trends in the south of the state that whetted his entrepreneurial appetite—namely, a relatively high percentage of people over sixty-five years of age who had retired there. Long Beach was typical of these new communities. Older persons had a habit of saving more than the general population and usually deposited a larger portion of their income in banks than did younger people. When A. P. scanned the statistics indicating growth in southern California, he found substantiation for his impressions. The number of building permits issued in Los Angeles between 1910 and 1915 was much higher than in San Francisco, while bank deposits and loans also doubled during these years.

Southern California seemed dynamic in so many ways. After 1909 the area was also experiencing an oil boom, which brought in substantial wealth. And the opening of the Panama Canal in 1914 provided an enormous boost to the state's economy and literally opened a new window on the commerce of the world. To celebrate access to new markets the Panama International Expositions in San Diego and San Francisco dramatized the new era and contributed to the upbeat mood of many Californians about their future. A. P. found the environment exhilarating. Together with Fagan he made an extensive tour through southern California in 1913 to observe its flowering at first hand and to plan strategies for participating in the boom.

Within a month after his arrival in Los Angeles in April 1913, A. P. had found a small weak bank that seemed ready to be absorbed. This was the Park Bank, which A. P. made into a new branch of the Bank of Italy. Local bankers did not welcome A. P.'s intrusion, however, and filed suits to stop him. Their efforts were not successful, and within a year he purchased three additional institutions. In each case he applied what by now emerged as the Giannini technique. As in San Jose, he created large advisory boards to which he appointed leading citizens of the community. In southern California, for example, he appointed W. C. Durgin, the former president of the Park Bank; Secondo Guasti, president of the Italian Vineyard Company; Giovannia Ferro, manager of the Schiappi Pietra Estate; and John Lagomarsino, president of the California Lima Beans Growers Association. He continued his maverick use of large-scale advertising. As he placed numerous notices in newspapers he extolled the virtues of savings accounts, and offered small loans to homeowners. "It is our purpose," A. P. announced, "to make a specialty of the interest of the small depositor and borrower. We aim to do all in our power to help in the building up of Los Angeles. . . . We have money to loan at all times to the man who wishes to build on property that he owns. We have no money for speculators. . . . We consider the wage earner or small business man who deposits his savings regularly, no matter how small the amount may be, to be the most valuable client our bank can have." In addition, he dispatched Armando Pedrini, now in charge of A. P.'s force of supersalesmen, into the community to use their high-pressure tactics for soliciting new accounts.

But southern California was in some ways unlike the north. For the first time A. P. found that his campaign was not working very well. During 1913 the economy was much softer in Los Angeles than in San Francisco. Despite the active sales pitch, A. P.'s staff was unable to increase deposits or loan applications. In fact, the new branches were incurring losses. Different also was the population base in the south. Most newcomers there were native-born midwesterners. In 1910, 53 percent of the people there were of native-born American parentage, compared with only 28 percent in San Francisco. And this group was obviously not attracted to the Bank of Italy, with its heavy sprinkling of Italian-Americans among staff and directors. In 1910 Los Angeles did not have very many Italians—only 3,802, compared to 16,918 in San Francisco. A. P. now realized that he could not build branches on the base of his Italian compatriots as he had up to now and that he had to devise different strategies to appeal to a more diversified clientele.

For the moment—but for the moment only—A. P. appeared defeated. A substantial number of his directors opposed his expansionist policies in the south and blamed him for the institution's losses. A. P. was deeply disappointed. On January 13, 1914, he therefore announced his intention to retire from the bank. "The burden of management," he declared, "had become too great for one in an exhausted physical state." He was to use this ploy at various times in his career. In the course of the year he recouped his energies, however, and succeeded in removing the dissidents from the board, which subsequently refused to accept his resignation. Happily for him, economic conditions also improved rapidly. The outbreak of the First World War created new markets for California's farmers, shipbuilders, and small manufacturers. A. P. met one of the first crises in his career in 1914 and managed to come out on top.

Thus encouraged, A. P. decided to resume his expansionist policies during the war years. Now that he had secured anchors for his projected empire in San Francisco and Los Angeles, he was determined to enter the area between them—the great San Joaquin Valley, three hundred miles long and forty miles wide. This was the largest and richest of California's agricultural valleys. Between 1916 and 1918 A. P. established ten new branches in the rural communities of this area. In the north he eyed likely spots in the wine country of the Sonoma and Napa valleys, utilizing his rapidly expanding network of advisory boards. He also secured eight new branches in urban centers. In each case he retained local advisers and employees and drew upon local capital and visibility as much as possible. Even so, it was usually not so much additional capital that he provided as managerial expertise. As his chauffeur drove him up and down California in his automobile, meeting new customers and employees, keeping a sharp lookout for possible acquisitions, this restless man could take satisfaction in having built a statewide system of branch banks in just one decade. As the fourth largest bank in California in 1918, he now presided over twenty-four branches in eighteen communities.

Without question, wartime economic conditions contributed greatly to his success. As A. P. noted in 1917: "Not until the spring of this year did the Coast awake to the evidences of a rapidly rising tide of war prosperity due to the unprecedented prices . . . for livestock and agricultural products. . . . No one could have foreseen the enormous increase in spring planting that followed the declaration of war. . . . The resulting crops that have been harvested this fall . . . give sensational evidence of what can be accomplished in the future."

Meanwhile, A. P.'s meteoric rise had begun to arouse fear and apprehension among the small bankers of the state. Just as the Southern Pacific Railroad had long had the image of an octopus in California (the term used by novelist Frank Norris in 1901 to describe its monopolistic hold on the economy), so now A. P.'s acquisitions had a similar effect. By the time he moved in to buy a potential institution for his system, he made arrangements that allowed him to drive a favorable bargain and to limit the options of the seller. At the behest of small bankers the American Bankers Association in 1916 had passed a resolution condemning branch banking. In that year only twelve states had laws allowing the practice, while twenty-seven others were silent on the matter, since it was not as yet an issue. Nine states explicitly prohibited it. Small bankers in California were obviously taken by surprise by the Bank of Italy's rapid expansion. As the *Coast Banker* noted in January 1918: "The rapidity with which he [A. P.] brought these institutions together has unquestionably been a matter of amazement to the banking public, and it is not exaggerating to say there has been a doubt in the minds of some bankers . . . as to the ability of the Bank of Italy to assimilate these institutions, hold them together, and develop them properly." By 1918 A. P. had become a threat to the status quo and the battle lines began to form.

With his sensitivity to politics, however, A. P. usually made sure that he would have powerful allies on his side, especially the state superintendent of banking. During the gubernatorial administration of the progressive Republican Hiram Johnson (1910–18), that individual was William R. Williams, an avowed advocate of banking reform. Although he had fined A. P. on various occasions for minor infractions of state banking laws, Williams favored the practice of branch banking. Like many progressives, he conceived of reform as embracing greater efficiency and rationality in business. That, to him, was more important than the possible threat of monopoly. Men like Williams represented the concepts of Theodore Roosevelt's New Nationalism, while small bankers were thinking more along the lines of President Wilson's New Freedom, which stressed opposition to monopoly and bigness.

Given this orientation, Williams approved A. P.'s applications for new branches. He elaborated on his thinking in 1916, when he wrote:

> Branch offices have been opened in places far removed from the principal place of business of the parent bank. . . . These branch offices offer to the communities in which they are greater assistance, larger loans, and more extended credit than local institutions can afford. The justification of their existence rests in this fact. . . . Still another cause has often influenced my course in granting the desired license. Occasionally it happens that the general banking tone of a community will measurably be improved by the licensing of a branch office of a well established, safely conducted institution.

Clearly, he was A. P.'s kind of man. When in 1918 the next governor, William D. Stephens, did not reappoint Williams, the latter resigned. Thereupon A. P. promptly hired him as cashier of the Bank of Italy. This aroused quite a few unfavorable comments and caused some embarrassment. But A. P. had a thick skin. "What if it does?" he asked. "Williams had the guts to clean up the banks of California, so I hired him to keep our bank clean."

The impact of the Bank of Italy's branch banks on the economy of California in the World War I era was considerable. In the first place, A. P. offered lower interest rates than other bankers. Agribusiness was already a major industry in the state, and California's commercial farmers had special credit needs. They required expensive irrigation equipment, built canals and ditches, bought intricate specialized machinery, and hired large gangs of field workers at various seasons. E. J. Wickson, a prominent agricultural economist, estimated in 1918 that even the average farmer in California needed at least $20,000 in credit yearly to operate successfully. As the *California Rural Press,* a leading farm periodical, reported on March 4, 1916, "In most localities the farmer . . . must pay a high rate of interest and in many cases is compelled to pay [in addition] a bonus to brokers. . . . There are many banks which refuse to loan directly upon country property but will loan upon the same property to a broker who charges from two to five per cent for his services." A. P. hoped to change this situation and to win thousands of such small farmers as his clients.

Most branches of the Bank of Italy were able to avoid some of the problems that had plagued smaller local banks. In general, its lending policies were more equitable and democratic. At other banks local merchants and financiers served on boards of directors who gave preference to their friends or to the important farmers or businessmen in their area. In addition, bank officers were often engaged in auxiliary enterprises, acting as grain merchants, cattle buyers, or real estate speculators. They usually had the most direct access to a bank's credit, leaving not much for others. By contrast, the Bank of Italy's policies were much more uniform. They were strictly supervised by the home office, which eschewed local favoritism and emphasized the impor- tance of small borrowers. And they were also much more able to meet varying seasonal requirements. In a sense, A. P. introduced a federal system, with fairly strong centralized control, but also a reasonable degree of local discretion. He coopted the bank officers he bought out and did not displace them. Although they gave up their independence, he endowed them with new titles, functions, and a range of perquisites.

A. P. sought to illustrate the differences between his and other banks by referring to the experience of his Santa Clara branch. As he reflected on it, he noted:

> When we bought the Santa Clara bank, the lending limit was $10,000. There happens to be a large business there which has seasonal require- ments running up to $200,000 or $250,000. . . . It was impossible for that business to satisfy its needs in the local field. . . . The moment we took . . . over, we were able to handle that business locally, and to extend the same lending facilities there as obtained everywhere else throughout our system.

A. P. designed the system so that each branch would be primarily sensitive to the seasonal needs of its particular area. The way James Bacigalupi, his legal counsel, explained it:

> Loans are made directly by the branches, except in instances where the amount is unusually large or the branch manager wishes to secure the advice of the head office credit department. The customers of the

branch deal with the local officers, and only in extraordinary circumstances are they brought into contact with the head office departments.
Each branch has a general lending limit fixed by the bank's finance
committee. Within this limit each branch may lend and report without
previous consultation with the head office. These limits vary with the
proven credit capacity of the various branch loaning officers. . . . All
applications for unfixed lines of credit in excess of the lending limits
of a given branch are promptly considered and acted upon by the
proper central credit departments and proper advice and instructions
issued. The broad fundamental policies respecting credits are outlined
by the general executive committee and application is then made by
the credit department.

Thus, each branch had the lending capacity of the central office,
subject to its performance record and certain broad limitations. The
system represented the essence of A. P.'s conception of the strengths
of branch banking as a form of banking and contained the administrative means that he devised to make that conception a functional
reality.

A. P.'s view of branch banking always reflected concern for the
small borrower. As his manager noted about A. P.'s branch in Mer-
ced, for example, "We had a lot of little farmers who needed money.
The branch grew because A. P. insisted that we take care of the little
farmer." In Madera, after only one year, the Bank of Italy branch had
garnered more than three-fourths of the accounts of small orchardists
in that locality.

A. P. also rigorously enforced prohibitions against conflicts of
interest by his managerial staff. In 1917, for example, he reduced the
salary of the manager of the Madera branch because he felt that the
man was devoting too much of his working time to the grain business.

A. P. relished publicizing his belief that the policies he followed
were beneficial not only to himself but for communities in the state.
Speaking to a local newspaperman in Fresno, he said, as reported in
the *Fresno Morning Republican,* October 20, 21, 1916:

> We believe that in having a prosperous surrounding country, the city
> will prosper and we also think that high rates of interest are ruinous
> to the farmers. We are here to make good times and . . . 7 percent will
> be our maximum rate of interest. [The Bank] is ready to loan
> $1,000,000 in the San Joaquin Valley and with resources of
> $32,000,000 . . . is in a position to negotiate a loan of any magnitude.
> . . . [Fresno] is a great undeveloped field . . . and that is the reason we
> are here. Fresno is as much our home as San Francisco, and we are
> going to do all possible in financial aid for the businessman and farmer.

In the decade after 1909 A. P. created a new banking empire. The rapid growth of the Bank of Italy was due to a number of factors that were rooted not only in A. P.'s extraordinary entrepreneurial talents but also in the dynamic nature of California's economy. One of A. P.'s major contributions was his insight into the development of a mass market. Unlike traditional bankers of his day, he perceived vast opportunities in mobilizing small depositors and borrowers and in actively soliciting their business. These included many immigrants and ethnic minorities who had not had experience with banks before and who needed to be educated in the ways of American finance. Perhaps because of his own immigrant background, he was particularly sensitive to their needs. As a first-generation American, he served as a guide to their acculturation into the byways of America's economic life.

To tap this vast market he was innovative in using unfamiliar methods. He relied on extensive advertising, long banking hours, courteous service, and the recruitment of a multilingual staff. Given his insight that large profits were to be made through quantity as well as quality, his emphasis on low interest rates fit well into his business scheme. He was as much an advocate of mass production in the field of banking as Henry Ford, his contemporary, was in the manufacture of automobiles. A. P. also emphasized an egalitarian approach to the bank's lending operations. Every potential customer, no matter how inexperienced or of limited means, was to be treated with courtesy and respect. This was in marked contrast to the loan policies of most contemporary bankers. In addition, the Bank of Italy with its branches had a flexibility that many other institutions lacked because it could shift its resources to areas of the state that needed them at various seasons of the year. The key to all of these policies was branch banking. By 1919 A. P. was more convinced than ever that it represented the wave of the future. With great resolution he now determined that he should extend it throughout the entire state, to the West as a region, to the nation, and, eventually, to the entire world. With such a vision, he embarked on a mission that provided him with an outlet for his nervous energies and gave a clear purpose to his life.

CHAPTER 3

The Great Expansion, 1919–1927

LIKE a military general mapping out strategy, A. P. in 1919 looked ahead to the expansion of his empire. He had accomplished laying of the groundwork for a statewide branch banking system. Now he hoped to increase its size and to render its operation more effective. The prospects seemed dazzling and tantalizing. But what he had not anticipated was a rising chorus of criticism and increasing opposition to his efforts. Other bankers and public regulators came to fear him as a monopolist, viewing him not as a constructive builder but as a ruthless manipulator who was undermining the independent smaller financiers of California. His creation of a highly centralized banking system evoked memories of the elder J. P. Morgan. During the 1920s, therefore, A. P. spent considerable energies in fighting off his enemies and became directly, and even embarrassingly, involved in politics.

Despite the battles, A. P. in the course of the decade succeeded in accomplishing most of his goals. By 1929 he had built a vast banking system, not only in California, but also in other western states, and had emerged as the West's undisputed leading banker. As the *San Francisco Chronicle* noted with pride on May 8, 1929: "A. P. Giannini is idolized today . . . because he was the first American to establish the West firmly on the map as a financial center to be reckoned with." How did he achieve this feat?

A. P.'s proverbial luck also stood him in good stead during the 1920s because, despite some ups and downs, the California economy still provided him with a positive environment for growth. Although much of the United States experienced depression conditions between 1919 and 1921, California remained more prosperous. Its farmers produced many more fruits and vegetables for urban markets than did their midwestern and southern counterparts. Consequently, they were far less affected by world competition and the fall of farm prices than those who were involved with grains, meat, and cotton. Moreover, since the West had little industry as yet, it was not as directly affected by declines of industrial production and unemployment as the Northeast. These conditions prevailed during much of the decade before 1929. No wonder, then, that banks in California did not experience quite as many difficulties as those elsewhere. Still, A. P. found the road to bigness strewn with obstacles and increasingly resorted to politics in an effort to remove them.

To provide his fledgling banks with greater status and national visibility in 1919, A. P. hoped to affiliate them with the Federal Reserve System, established in 1914. He admired it in part because in his eyes it was a national version of branch banking. Moreover, membership would increase the prestige of his institutions and was likely to increase the volume of their business. It would also allow greater flexibility of operation than was possible under state charters. He also foresaw legal advantages, especially in easing the acquisition of new banks.

A. P., however, wanted to join only on his terms, and he hesitated because of two impediments. In the first place, California banking laws required that state banks deposit two sets of reserves, one in the Federal Reserve Bank, and another to meet state requirements. This was an onerous burden and initially led only four California banks to join the system. A. P. felt that this was more than he could afford. Second, he wanted an advance commitment from the Federal Reserve Board approving branch banking. His was now the fourth largest bank organization in the state, and he knew that Federal Reserve officials were eager to have him in their fold.

Since he was not of the bashful sort, A. P. relayed his concerns to Washington, D.C., and to Sacramento. Negotiations began in the fall of 1917, when Adolph C. Miller, a governor of the Federal Reserve Board, came to visit him to discuss specific terms. Miller placed A. P.'s views before the entire board, who largely agreed to his demands. As Miller wrote to A. P. on September 26, 1917: "The Board is not opposed to the principle of branch banking. . . . The sole concern . . . will be to satisfy itself that any proposed extension will not impair . . . the safety of your institution. . . . It would be a great pleasure personally to see your bank blazing the way in your state and setting a much needed example by taking membership in the Federal Reserve." That response cleared the way for A. P., but he was still concerned about the reserve requirements. Along with other bankers in the California Bankers Association, he lobbied hard in Sacramento between 1917 and 1919 to repeal the separate state restrictions. The association had considerable influence with the lawmakers, who in 1919 obligingly repealed the objectionable provision. When the law became operative on July 22, 1919, the Bank of Italy and ten other state-chartered banks in California applied for Federal Reserve membership and were readily accepted. In many ways this step reflected the maturation of A. P.'s system and gave him added stature as one of the more creative bankers in the United States.

In the 1920s A. P. found that he had to spend much more time dealing with political problems than in his earlier banking career. As long as he had been a small and rather obscure financier, he had experienced relatively few difficulties with California state officials concerning his plans for expansion. But now that he was becoming known as the West's premier advocate of branch banking, his activities were in the limelight. No longer did he represent the "little guy" in California banking. Many of the small bankers feared that branches would drain funds from rural areas to big cities. And, quite accurately, they expected the Bank of Italy would drive them out of business. As one independent banker put it, branch banking was "in essence monopolistic . . . and steps should be taken now to eradicate it before a condition develops which would invite great harm to individuals and communities." A banker from Fresno called the Bank of Italy "undemocratic and an alien innovation from Europe." It threatened the "American way" of banking. "The traditional small-town banker was temperamentally in better tune with the small businessman of his small town and with the farmer than the directors of a rich and powerful bank whose head office is in San Francisco." A few critics reflected the nativist prejudice of the era. They charged that the Vatican secretly owned the bank. In February 1922 the editor of the *Coast Banker* investigated the accusation. He found no basis in it and also reported that A. P. employed more Masons and Protestants than Catholics. Whatever the nature of the accusations, however, A.P.'s image in the 1920s was more that of a giant monopolist who was seeking to bring a large share of bank deposits in California under his control.

Certainly that was the impression of Charles F. Stern, the new state bank superintendent, who assumed his position in 1918. Stern had served very capably as state highway commissioner in the reform administration of progressive governor Hiram Johnson. He had little experience in banking but had served as campaign manager for William D. Stephens, Johnson's successor in 1918. A former Congressman and mayor of Los Angeles, Stephens had also served as president of the Los Angeles Chamber of Commerce. Like many Los Angeles businessmen, he was apprehensive about A. P.'s expansion of branch banks there. Nor was he enamored of A. P. personally. A. P. had doggedly pursued him in collecting an unpaid loan Stephens had taken out at the Park Bank, an institution that was absorbed in the Bank of Italy system. Stephens appointed Stern as his bank superintendent. Stern's critics charged that he knew little about banking and that he received advice from his hometown banker, C. F. Gorman of Eureka, California. Whether or not there was substance to the rumor, Stern was too intelligent a public official to be influenced solely by any one individual. In his concerns about branch banking he reflected the apprehensions of a great many Californians, apprehensions that at the time seemed entirely legitimate.

After making a thorough examination of banking conditions in California, Stern concluded that the Bank of Italy's expansion was too rapid. He first broached his concerns in a long letter that he sent to A. P. on June 23, 1919, in which he questioned many of A. P.'s policies. "The Bank of Italy is unique in American banking," Stern declared quite aptly. "Your progress has been so rapid . . . the units added to your organization have been so numerous and so widely scattered, that the general situation . . . raises two distinct questions of paramount importance." Stern then wondered whether it was proper for the bank to have branches "in territory without close economic relationship to your home office." In addition, he pointed to numerous questions of loose administration and minor infractions of existing state bank laws. Stern felt that A. P.'s bank was not well integrated. "Your branch offices are neither absorbed nor assimilated," he charged. "We are not only disappointed, but we are very seriously concerned . . . from the standpoint of the safety and ultimate solvency of your institution. . . . You indulge a practice vicious from every point of view, by paying dividends upon the basis of interest discount uncollected, thus misrepresenting the actual status of your affairs and invading your capital." Under such circumstances it was not surprising that he denied A. P. permission to open a new branch.

Stern was reflecting not only Governor Stephens's concerns about A. P. but also those of many small bankers in the state. Looking back on his actions a quarter of a century later, Stern said: "When I became superintendent, I ran into a whispering campaign against the Bank of Italy. Bankers beat a path to my office to explain about the monopolistic tendency of the bank. They complained about its aggressive methods, saying that it was getting so big it could do anything it desired to a competing bank. The Los Angeles banks complained about a bank from San Francisco spreading itself over the south, and the more I thought about it, the clearer it became to me that the south should be left to southern bankers and northern bankers should stay in their part of the state."

Although A. P.'s legendary temper flared, he hoped to avoid a direct confrontation. Thus he sent his cashier, William Williams, the former state superintendent of banking, together with legal counsel James Bacigalupi, to confer with Stern. As the two entered his office, Stern maintained a serious mien. As Bacigalupi remembered the meeting: "Stern declared that branch banking was Canadian and European in principle and did not suit the temperament of our people. He said it was monopolistic, likely to control the finances and politics of a whole state; that [it] had inherent weakness because of its spread-out condition, and he likened it to 'a house of cards.' " Before Williams and Bacigalupi left the room, Stern added that "so long that he was superintendent of banking, we could hope for no permission to expand."

Meanwhile, A. P. found it increasingly difficult to control his anger. When he did not express it to those around him, he used the pages of the bank's house organ, *Bankitaly Life,* to transmit his defiance. He rejected all criticisms of his bank, unlike his subordinates who admitted some looseness of administration. To him the Federal Reserve Board's admission of his banks into its system represented an endorsement of his banking practices—which, in truth, it was not. A. P. decried the "open hostility to our further expansion" but vowed in no way to sway from his course. "Nothing," he declared, "will deter [the bank] from lawfully benefiting the residents of any and every part of California."

Stern maintained his calm and took his stand on issues of public policy, particularly the pervasive fear of monopoly. Although admitting "the unquestioned benefit your branch offices have brought to many specific localities, I cannot believe that the . . . public advantage . . . can be promoted by a theory of banking that, when its ultimate has been reached, four or three or one Bank of Italy controls the finance of California. . . . You express the utmost confidence that your organization has wiped out time and distance and is operating your organization as a unit; I express the doubt whether, in view of the different economic problems . . . and the physical separation [of branches], you are so operating." In view of these reservations, which he expressed in November 1919, Stern declared, "You may not go forward with further [branch] expansion, but you may rely on the department for every support in your problems of correlation and digestion."

But A. P. now developed methods to bypass the state banking superintendents, methods he was to develop extensively throughout the decade. Because he had just joined the Federal Reserve System, he could buy or absorb banks with national rather than state charters, since the jurisdiction of state officials was restricted to California. So he organized a new corporation, the Stockholders Auxiliary, which became his immediate tool for the purchase of new banks. And purchase new banks he did. Within two years he bought ten more institutions, some in rural communities like Sunnyvale and Hayward, and four more in San Francisco. Although he did not immediately transform them into branches, they were, as one of his aides admitted, "in all but name only . . . branches of the Bank of Italy."

Those who already had some concerns about A. P. now became even more suspicious because he seemed to be operating outside the law. As one critic noted, his actions "increased the fear and mystification people in California felt about Giannini, who seemed to be operating sub rosa—through secret agents." By 1921 A. P. had increased deposits by $42 million and counted 200,000 depositors. Clearly, he was accomplishing some of his broad goals. He had built the largest bank west of Chicago, and he had a larger number of depositors than any other bank in the United States. His ruthlessness and drive as well as his extraordinary talents as a banker were beginning to become legendary. As the *San Francisco Chronicle* commented on December 25, 1920: "By every sign the really frightening thing to his competitors is that Giannini's drive for the financial domination of California is only just getting under way."

Moreover, the global scale of A. P.'s ambitions became quite evident in the postwar era (1919–21). When A. P. spoke to the Italian chamber of commerce in New York City in 1918, he told them bluntly that if they would raise $1.5 million to purchase a bank, he would agree to manage it. As he instructed his emissaries who were to work out details—his brother Attilio and legal counsel Bacigalupi—he hoped to exploit the mass market, especially "the foreign elements—

Italians, Greeks, Poles, Swiss, Slavonians, Spanish, etc.!" They were also to consult community leaders, lawyers, doctors, and important bankers like J. P. Morgan, Jr. In addition, "it may be well to bring out in your talks the possibility of . . . going to Italy to establish branches of [an] affiliated institution . . . after it has made good in New York." And then he advised them to use his management style in the East. "There is one thing, Jim," he instructed Bacigalupi, "and that is if we would have anything to do with . . . [a bank] in New York, we would see to it that the managing officers, from the president down, were put out in front and in the open where they would come in contact with and greet the people as they would come in or go out of the bank. . . . That is one thing that is lacking in most of the New York banking institutions. We certainly do not want our officers cooped up in an office." A. P.'s negotiations were successful. In 1919 he purchased the East River National Bank as his first eastern outpost. Within a year he also bought the Banc dell' Italia Meridionale in Italy, which gave him a direct branch outlet in Europe.

It should be noted that A. P. was not the only branch banker in California. Others were experimenting with the technique between 1919 and 1929, although perhaps not quite to the same extent as he. Among those who were significant was Joseph F. Sartori of the Security Trust Company in Los Angeles, A. P.'s leading competitor in the south. The Mercantile Trust Company, the American Bank of San Francisco, and the First National Bank of Los Angeles also created branches during the 1920s, although these were usually within city limits, and not on a statewide basis such as those of A. P. Next to Sartori, probably Henry Robinson of the Pacific Southwest was A. P.'s most formidable rival. Robinson was also a power in California's Republican Party and a close friend of Herbert Hoover. A. P. did not relish their competition, especially since he felt that they were using Superintendent Stern to block his own expansionist efforts. Between 1919 and 1920 Stern granted a total of seventy-one permits for new branches, of which A. P. received only two, and these were simply for moving existing banks across the street to new locations. A. P. took Stern's actions personally and became convinced that Stern was an agent of Sartori and Robinson, who were opposing A. P.'s entry into southern California. He was always one who feared conspiracies. "They're trying to limit us," he told his associates, "and then cut us up into little pieces." His suspicions were confirmed in

1921, when Stern resigned his post as state superintendent of banking to become a senior vice-president of Robinson's Pacific Southwest Bank.

At the same time, in June of 1921, A. P. moved the Bank of Italy's headquarters to a new seven-story building at One Powell Street, in the heart of San Francisco's financial district. In keeping with his new status as one of California's largest bankers—with forty-one branches in thirty localities—A. P. directed the decoration of a large marble tiled lobby with an immense fifty-ton steel and concrete vault, a far cry from the one he had placed on his fruit and vegetable wagon during the San Francisco earthquake just fifteen years earlier. Many San Franciscans took pride in the structure, the largest exclusively devoted to banking in North America. A. P. himself felt some nostalgic qualms, however, which he kept largely to himself, qualms about moving away from his roots in San Francisco's Italian community. "When I moved up there," he said, "I experienced the only fear I ever experienced in business. I had a sinking feeling . . . wondering whether I made a blunder moving from the place where all my success had been laid. I wondered if old friends and associates would believe we were mainly putting on the dog."

Doubts did not prevent him from continuing to press for expansion, however. When in June 1921 the legislature adjourned without taking any restrictive action against branch banking, A. P. thought it a good omen and promptly applied to Stern for eight new branches. Two days before he left his office, on June 18, 1921, Stern reversed his earlier opposition and gave A. P. all of the desired outlets. He defended his action by noting that A. P. had solved problems of coordination. Since the lawmakers had refused to restrict branch expansion, Stern concluded that "it is fair to assume that California is now committed to this [statewide] type of banking." When Stern resigned, Governor Stephens replaced him with Jonathan Dodge, a prominent Los Angeles attorney and former banker who had served as chairman of that city's Board of Supervisors.

A. P. was greatly encouraged by these developments and speeded up the pace of his acquisitions. Two weeks after Dodge assumed office A. P. sent him an application for a new branch in Sacramento, the state capital. Just a year before, Stern had rejected a similar application. To develop a favorable image A. P. himself went to Sacramento and helped to float a new municipal bond issue for a city filtration plant. He hoped to impress Dodge about the beneficial impact of a Bank of Italy branch in the community. He also dispatched twenty-nine employees from the home office to the city to solicit signatures of local citizens desiring a branch. They scoured streets and back alleys and collected eight thousand such signatures urging the superintendent to issue a permit. Without hesitation, Dodge approved the request and in July 1921 granted A. P. three additional branches. That encouraged A. P. to go on a veritable shopping spree in August, when he purchased six new banks that were part of the Rideout chain in the Sacramento Valley.

Small independent bankers could see the handwriting on the wall and worried about their possible demise. During the second half of 1922 more than five hundred of them organized the California League of Independent Bankers. They took an oath not to sell any of their banks to A. P. But their main goal was to form a strong lobby that would press the legislature to limit branch banking in the state. In addition, they embarked on a publicity campaign, using lecturers and advertisements that warned Californians about the evils of monopoly in banking and hinted at the un-American nature of branch banks. As the league declared in one of its publications: "Our independent banks have been one of the best supports of the true principles of American democracy. They have done more to upbuild this powerful nation than all the cream-skimming banks have done for other nations."

In the nativist atmosphere of the immediate postwar years, attacks on A. P. occasionally had antiforeign overtones. On one occasion, the leading fundamentalist radio preacher in southern California, "Fighting Bob" Shuler, directly attacked A. P. "There is no question but what the Bank of Italy was founded and is controlled and is officered by Roman Catholic Italians," he declared. "It is generally known that by some slick work they have gained control of most of the banks and financial institutions of California. . . . The Bank of Italy is well on its way to consummating its plan toward controlling the entire West, both financially and politically."

The complaints of the independent bankers gave pause to Dodge. No other financier in the state seemed as bent on rapid acquisitions as A. P. And as Dodge looked more closely into Bank of Italy operations, he found some cause for concern. The accounting department was far behind in documenting recent acquisitions and in providing the state with accurate information. New branches were often left to their own devices for many months because the main office was too busy with other problems to provide much supervision. Bank statements the institution sent to the superintendent were often incomplete and did not supply important data. Without question, at times A. P.'s management style was high-handed and autocratic. "The directors function in a perfunctory manner," Dodge complained in 1922. At meetings "their attendance is poor." Pointing an accusing finger at A. P., he noted that "as a result the management of your affairs is dominated by what may be termed your official family. This control is held so closely by President Giannini and his immediate associates that insofar as such a thing is possible in an institution of your size, your management may be likened to the well-known one-man bank." This was in September 1921. Consequently Dodge refused to grant permits for new branches until A. P. cleaned his house and corrected existing weaknesses.

A. P. was especially dismayed by Dodge's charges because they alerted the Federal Reserve Board in Washington and seemed to indicate that not all was well in his banking empire. Dodge sent copies of his correspondence with A. P. and Bank of Italy officials to John Perrin, the chairman of the Federal Reserve Bank of San Francisco, as well as to the Federal Reserve Board in Washington. There officials decided they would act in concert with the California state superintendent and, for the moment, would withhold approval of applications for new branches that A. P. might make.

A. P., however, was already making plans to bypass Dodge. When he opened his new headquarters building, he closed his old Market Street branch. But he figured he might use these premises to open a new bank with a national rather than a state charter, which would not require state permission. Thus he went ahead with this venture without even applying for federal approval because he was sure he could receive that, once his bank was already in operation. But John Perrin was furious about this devious maneuver. When he contacted his superiors in Washington, he recommended against issuance of a national bank charter to A. P. because he opposed the Bank of Italy's ownership of a string of banks through an affiliate, or through indirect holding companies as A. P. was suggesting.

Somewhat stymied, A. P. turned to another subterfuge. He now decided to organize the new bank as an independent state-chartered institution (not a branch) and proceeded to do that on August 8, 1921. That antagonized Perrin even further. He announced that in the future it would be necessary to secure "approval of the Federal Reserve Board, at least tentatively, before proceeding to acquire any bank for the Bank of Italy, or any corporation affiliated with it." Since the Bank of Italy was now a member of the Federal Reserve System, its purchases of other banks by its holding companies were subject to federal approval. That was a restriction A. P. had not anticipated when he first joined the system. But Perrin was supported by Federal Reserve governor W. P. G. Harding, who wrote A. P. that the board would take no action on any of his new purchases until it had "definite advice from you as to the maximum number of branches it is contemplated that the Bank of Italy shall have."

A. P. was a hard man to keep down, for now he decided to use political influence to achieve his objectives. Already for some years he had indulged in the practice of hiring public officials for his bank, paying them ample salaries and then using them to negotiate with the public agencies with which they had formerly been associated. That was how he had secured former state superintendent William A. Williams in 1918, and how he utilized John S. Chambers, the former state controller of California, who managed his Sacramento branch. Now, in his tiff with the Federal Reserve Board, he hired William G. McAdoo as special counsel. McAdoo, Woodrow Wilson's son-in-law, had been secretary of the treasury under Wilson and a member of the Federal Reserve Board. McAdoo began a series of conferences with Perrin and with Federal Reserve officials in Washington to quiet their fears. After ironing out various procedural problems, McAdoo negotiated an agreement between A. P. and the Federal Reserve Board. Concluded in January 1922, this stipulated that the board would grant licenses to the more than two dozen branches A. P. had bought in the previous two years. In turn, he promised to seek their approval for new branches in the future. As McAdoo worded the document:

> The Bank of Italy agrees that for the future it will not either directly or indirectly, through affiliated corporations or otherwise, acquire an interest in another bank in excess of 20 percent or indirectly promote the establishment of any new bank for the purpose of acquiring such an interest in it, nor make any engagement to acquire such an interest without first having received the approval of the Federal Reserve Board, following an application on a form approved by said Board.

Yet A. P. was already dreaming of new and legal ways to circumvent this agreement as he sailed off to Europe for a year. As he told one of his subordinates: "If you can't do a thing one way, you do it another way."

Meanwhile, State Superintendent Dodge was trying to cope with the pressures both from A. P. and from the California League of Independent Bankers. In seeking to work out a compromise, in December 1921 he issued the de novo rule. Under this guideline, he made a distinction between the purchase of existing banks and the chartering of brand new branches. The latter were to be permitted only in the home cities of parent institutions. Elsewhere, existing banks would have to be acquired. However, Dodge explained to A. P., "this rule will be subject to exceptions." A. P. vigorously protested the new policy, which he believed benefited his competitors in the south, and lost no time in trying to use the loophole for exceptions.

But economic conditions in California favored the spread of branch banking and worked in A. P.'s favor. The seasonal requirements of big agribusiness absorbed increasingly large amounts of capital—demands that independent small bankers were often unable to provide. Only larger and more heavily capitalized institutions could shift their resources to various parts of the state as conditions required. That situation was dramatized in March of 1924 when the Valley Bank of Fresno, with eight branches, was on the verge of failure because of poor management. Its collapse threatened to precipitate a financial crisis in California. Both the state superintendent of banking and the Federal Reserve Board hoped to avert such a debacle. It seemed that the only alternative was to have the institution taken over by two of the strongest banks in the state, the Bank of Italy and the Pacific Southwest Bank. Although A. P. was not overly anxious to absorb the properties in Fresno, where he already had branches, they gave him an important political advantage, since both the state superintendent and the Federal Reserve Board were now willing to suspend their earlier restrictions on the extension of his branches.

Nevertheless, A. P. developed still additional strategies to facilitate his program of expansion. By 1924 he had decided to ignore the agreement with the Federal Reserve Board that he signed in 1922. He formed a new holding company that was designed to become the prime instrument for the purchase of additional banks. This was the Bancitaly Corporation, at the time a small holding company that owned the stock of his modest banks in New York City and in Italy. In 1924 he moved Bancitaly's headquarters from New York to Los Angeles. And to dramatize his intentions of becoming a major force in southern California, he built a new twelve-story Bank of Italy building in Los Angeles at Seventh and Olive streets in the heart of the downtown section. And soon he began to use Bancitaly to make new purchases. That he could do without Federal Reserve Board approval, since his instrument had a very different group of stockholders than the Bank of Italy. Legally it was a separate entity. Within a year, he bought two dozen banks through Bancitaly, of which eleven were in Los Angeles. A. P. had arrived in southern California, and he was there to stay.

A. P. then decided to extend his devious strategy further. He decided to use other subsidiaries as well, in which he would play a silent role. In 1924 he purchased one of the most successful state-chartered banks in Los Angeles, the Bank of America. A. P. signed an agreement with its president, Ora Monette, to form another legal entity, the Americommercial Corporation, of which Monette became president. A. P. held no office in this firm, but Bancitaly owned all of its stock and operated it as a subsidiary. In the booming Los Angeles real estate market, which Monette knew well, it became exceedingly profitable. Before the end of 1925 it had thirty-five branches in Los Angeles and its environs and fulfilled the hopes A. P. had for his bypass strategy.

Such was A. P.'s ego, however, that he found it difficult to wage his battle for expansion quietly without direct frontal attacks on those he believed to be his adversaries. Feeling confident in 1924, he decided to challenge the state superintendent of banks directly because the superintendent was loath to give him completely free access to the establishment of unlimited numbers of branches in the south. The individual in question was the incumbent, John F. Johnson (1923–25), a former state superintendent of education. Although relatively inexperienced in banking matters, Johnson was sympathetic to some of A. P.'s critics around the state who viewed the Bank of Italy's policies with alarm and feared its apparent tendency toward monopoly. Between 1923 and 1925 Johnson issued fifty-four permits for branches to A. P.'s competitors, who were taking advantage of Los Angeles's rapid growth. During that same period Johnson permitted A. P. only one branch there. That angered A. P. no end, who perceived himself the object of discrimination.

Consequently A. P. decided to contest the de novo rule openly and to demand state approval of new branches. In addition, A. P. hoped to persuade the legislature in 1924 to amend the State Banking Act of 1909. He proposed that the state superintendent of banking be required to issue permits for new branches whenever 20 percent of registered voters in a community signed a petition requesting one. This suggestion elicited strong opposition from bankers in the south and from the California League of Independent bankers and went down to defeat.

Stymied by the legislature and the state superintendent, A. P. now attempted a third method of attack: the use of the courts. The specific challenge came from Superintendent Johnson, who refused to issue A. P. a permit to establish a branch near the new Los Angeles Civic Center, which was under construction in 1925. A. P. had been operating a branch at the site before the buildings on it were razed. It had been the hub of an old Italian neighborhood. A. P. wanted his branch to follow the population, which moved a few blocks to the north. When Johnson refused to grant the necessary license, A. P. instructed his lawyers to apply to the California Supreme Court for a writ of mandamus that would force the superintendent to issue a permit. But after extensive legal wrangling the judges concluded that A. P. had not been the victim of a conspiracy as he had charged and refused to issue the necessary order.

This setback led A. P. to attempt an even bolder move—to challenge the regional restrictions that the superintendent had placed on his expansion. In his effort to bring the Bank of America of Los Angeles north to the San Francisco area in January 1925, he applied to Johnson for acquiring a branch in Chico, north of San Francisco. Johnson rejected the application because the area was not contiguous to Los Angeles and reiterated his policy of allowing branch banking only in well-defined zones of the state in the north and south.

The decision infuriated A. P. but merely encouraged him to try other diversions. He renewed his application but this time used his Liberty Bank of San Francisco as the main sponsoring institution. That application Johnson could not reject, since it fell within established policy.

In addition, A. P. demanded that the superintendent allow him to consolidate his sprawling banks. He had now built four separate branch-banking systems. These included the Bank of Italy, Bancitaly (a holding company), the Liberty Bank of San Francisco, and the Bank of America in Los Angeles. To unite all four he required approval of the Federal Reserve Board for the first two (members of the Federal Reserve System) and the California state banking superintendent for the others. On November 30, 1925, A. P. applied to Johnson to unite the Liberty Bank and the Bank of America. By now his empire contained 155 branches with deposits in excess of $464 million. It was the dominant banking system in California.

Supremely confident, A. P. was not psychologically prepared for Johnson's opposition. Although the superintendent approved thirty-one of his applications for additional branches, he openly expressed his concerns. On March 5, 1926, he wrote A. P. a seventeen-page letter in which he questioned the latter's motives. As he noted:

> Is it not a fact that Bancitaly Corporation will, if and when its full purpose is accomplished, be in control of the largest, most scattered, and diversified, and most difficult to control chain banking system so far devised? We ask you . . . to inform us how it is possible . . . to know what the condition of the chain is, and even if it were able [for the state Banking Department] to put its finger on a weak link in this chain, what control it would have over the situation, and what remedy it would be possible to apply?
>
> Is it the intention of your banks . . . to circumvent the law when it stands in the way of your expansion, by doing indirectly what cannot be done directly? Is it your intention . . . to thus attempt a monopoly of the banking business of the State of California? Do your intentions go further in this regard, and if so are they of national or international scope?
>
> Kindly state, also, at what point, if any, short of the elimination of the independent banker, you propose to stop?

A. P. was stunned and had his staff prepare a reply, which came to fifty-eight pages. The Banking Act of 1909 did not authorize "an exercise of power by the Superintendent . . . of the type or kind implied by his letter. Therefore, the Superintendent's duty . . . is to approve the consolidation without further ado or delay." A. P. returned early from a European trip to lead the attack.

After contemplating the situation carefully, A. P. decided that he would have to enter politics directly to break the impasse. He was persuaded by the recommendations of his chief advisers that he should take a direct part in the upcoming gubernatorial election in the state. Thus A. P. carefully pondered the attitudes of the four leading gubernatorial candidates in the Republican primary (Californians tended to vote Republican in these years). One was Friend Richardson, the incumbent who sought reelection. A. P. opposed him because he had appointed Johnson as state bank superintendent. A second candidate was Judge Rex B. Goodcell, supported by business interests. A. P. knew him but was not overly keen, although A. P. contributed $5,000 to his campaign fund, just in case. Two other strong contenders included Lieutenant governor C. C. Young, and State School Superintendent Will C. Wood. All of them, except Wood, approached the Bank of Italy for support. As vice-president and legal adviser, James Bacigalupi wrote to A. P.: "It is deplorable that we should be forced into politics . . . but there are times when it is better to have fought and lost than not to have fought at all. . . . I think that you personally should . . . come out openly for Young. Let us take a stand and give them the best we have. . . . You are the *Big Chief,* and we anxiously await your orders."

A. P. did not need much persuasion. "We had to fight," he said. "If Richardson had been reelected, we would have had to undergo four more years of political domination, and our development would have been held back that much." By August 24 he openly gave out the word that he was supporting Young, although the latter refused to take any public stand on the banking controversy and made no open commitments. Nevertheless, A. P. instructed his branch managers and all of his employees to bend all efforts to elect Young. In the ensuing months thousands of them became involved in the campaign. The Richardson supporters were outraged. "California does not need a Mussolini," one of their broadsides proclaimed. The ensuing primary election was very close, but Young won the nomination by twelve thousand votes. A. P. was elated. "There was certainly never a more loyal bunch in the world than the Bank of Italy family," he gloated.

A. P.'s political interference aroused much unfavorable comment throughout the state. Harrison Chandler's *Los Angeles Times* revealed that A. P. had contributed $150,000 to the Young campaign. As the newspaper declared: "The contest for the Republican nomination has been invaded by a powerful banker, A. P. Giannini. He wants an official who will give him what Governor Richardson has refused— special privileges and favors. If Young is elected, Banker Giannini expects to be the financial dictator of California." The caption to this statement announced that "California does not need a Mussolini, financial, political, or otherwise."

With Young's subsequent election as governor in November, A. P. had high hopes that he could continue the consolidation of his banking system. Initially the new chief executive maintained a discreet silence. Meanwhile, A. P. embarked on another surge of bank purchases in the expectation that soon he could consolidate them all into one large system. In January 1927 his Bancitaly bought twenty-eight institutions. Before that month was out, however, Young appointed a new bank superintendent. He was Will C. Wood, the former state superintendent of education, who had no connection to the industry and was supposedly impartial.

A. P. immediately confronted Wood. On Wood's second day in office he was visited by Bacigalupi and Vice-President W. R. Williams of the Bank of Italy. They presented him not only with the application for the merger of the Bank of America of Los Angeles with the Liberty Bank (which Johnson had denied) but also with an additional sixty sales and purchase agreements. A day later Williams returned seeking thirty-eight permits in addition for de novo branches in Los Angeles. Wood was flabbergasted and bewildered. As he remembered the occasion in later years, Williams walked in, shook his hand, and peremptorily demanded a decision. "Here I was inexperienced in my new office," Wood reminisced, "without technical knowledge of banking, facing decisions on an application that if granted would create a giant bank. Two men, representing a giant financial interest, sat with eyes fixed on me to catch an intimation of my intention regarding their application. I had been urged to grant it; urged not to grant it. The governor had told me distinctly that I was under no obligation to grant the merger. . . . All these things flashed through my mind as I sat there, with three [sic] pairs of eyes fixed on me."

Wood dallied only briefly, referring the applications to his legal department. After a week they informed him that he had a wide range of options. Meanwhile, the visits by Bank of Italy officials continued, as A. P. kept up the pressure. On January 26, 1927, less than a month after he took office, Wood approved the merger of A. P.'s banks. They now became the Liberty Bank of America, with 136 branches and $200 million in assets. Wood noted that in the previous year his predecessor had approved seven similar mergers for other banks. In all fairness, therefore, he felt he could not deny the Bank of Italy's application. He also abrogated the de novo rule and granted the Liberty Bank nineteen new branches. A. P.'s involvement in politics had obviously been a great success and had removed impediments to his consolidation efforts at the state level.

Many Californians took pride in his accomplishment. As the *San Francisco Examiner* noted: "Here is an enormous financial institution founded and fostered on the soil of California. Banking in this country and abroad had its great families: the Rothschilds, the Morgans, the Mitsui. This Californian, Giannini, is the first financier to make of banking and investments [a] huge democratic fraternity." Understandably, Italian-Americans took special pride in the meteoric rise of one of their own. "I was a dago before Giannini," one told a Boston reporter. "Now I am an American."

While A. P. was conducting an active campaign for consolidation in California, he also opened a second front in Washington, D.C. Since some of his banks were members of the Federal Reserve System, he needed approval from the Federal Reserve Board to unite his disparate properties. In 1924 the board was still divided over the extension of branch banking. A majority of four members joined Comptroller of the Currency Charles G. Dawes in opposing it. Dawes hoped to strengthen the national bank system at a time when it was in decline. Many national banks were leaving it and obtaining state charters because these afforded them more liberal and flexible rules for operation. The minority, however, believed that if the board loosened curbs on branch banking by national banks, that would tempt them to remain in the system. That position was also held by Senator Carter Glass in Congress (the father of the Federal Reserve System), who in February 1924 successfully defeated efforts to curb branch banking.

At this stage A. P.'s legendary luck came to the rescue. Dawes resigned as comptroller in 1925 and was succeeded by Joseph W. McIntosh, who had a rather benign view of branch banking. In the summer of 1925 McIntosh made a trip to California to observe branch banking at first hand. While there he also met with A. P., who recited a long list of what he perceived as alleged injustices he had endured. In particular, he urged McIntosh to reconsider a proposed acquisition (Santa Maria), which the Federal Reserve Board had earlier rejected. McIntosh was sympathetic and in ensuing months sent two examiners to investigate this local situation. Their recommendation was that the board grant A. P. his desired branch. A. P. felt vindicated. As he wrote to a friend with jubilation: "They are extremely pleased with the manner in which we conduct our business. Many of them were under the impression that we run a sloppy institution, but they have come to the realization that there are very few institutions in the country that can compare with us."

A. P. now stepped up the pressure to secure federal approval for his planned grand consolidation. Moreover, by 1925 McIntosh was arguing that the unification of A. P.'s banks would simplify the task of regulators and was winning a majority on the Federal Reserve

Board. Throughout that year A. P. and he were conducting negotiations, while the board now looked on branch bank expansion favorably. They approved three new branches for him in northern California and eleven additional ones in the southern part of the state. In January 1926, as A. P. was anticipating board approval of his consolidation, he secured their assent to another twenty-eight branches, which he rushed to include before his planned major reorganization. Not long thereafter the board voted to give their approval to the merger.

Meanwhile, A. P.'s lieutenants in Washington were lobbying for legislation to expand permissible operations for national banks, which would make his own institutions in that system more profitable. The McFadden Bill in Congress was designed to accomplish that goal. It proposed to allow national banks to make extended real estate loans (for five years rather than one), to expand legal lending limits on farm loans, to allow the addition of savings departments and safe-deposit facilities, and to issue perpetual rather than ninety-nine-year charters for trust operations. With intensive pressure from the Bank of Italy, Congress enacted the measure on February 25, 1927. At the same time, Comptroller McIntosh insisted on receiving a pledge from A. P. that Bancitaly would not own more than 25 percent of the capital stock of the Bank of Italy for the next five years. A. P. consented reluctantly because he needed McIntosh's support for Federal Reserve Board approval of his reorganization. And he could afford to be generous because the union of his banks made his the largest bank in the West and the third largest bank in the nation (behind National City and Chase National banks in New York). By 1927 A. P. had accumulated 276 branches in 199 localities.

But it was in A. P.'s restless nature that he consistently sought new challenges and dreamed new dreams. Now that he had built the largest network of interrelated banks in California and the West in a little more than two decades, he looked for even greater frontiers to conquer. Perhaps he could extend his empire on a national scale, to embrace a nationwide system of branch banks. Or possibly he could establish the nation's largest bank. Beyond such visions lay the possibility of creating a global banking system. To A. P. the opportunities seemed infinite.

Even in 1927 A. P.'s restlessness was not assuaged by the grandiose merger that resulted in the Bank of Italy National Trust and Savings Association. He himself felt that the system was not as comprehensive as he would have liked. And he set himself the goal of having at least one of his branches in every California town. At the same time he could not forget that Canada already had a nationwide chain of branch banks, an example he hoped to emulate in the United States. If he was to cross state lines, however, he needed to secure amendments to the McFadden Act, which limited banks to operations within the confines of a single state. In 1927, therefore, he mounted a new lobbying campaign in Congress for an amendment that would permit branch banking on a national scale.

In line with this objective A. P. again reverted to the use of political influence. He hired Charles W. Collins as a consultant. Collins had served as deputy comptroller of the currency in 1925 and had been the major draftsman of the early version of the McFadden Act. By 1927 Collins had resigned his position with the federal government to become a private bank consultant. A. P. also turned to him for advice in interpreting the McFadden Act, especially in respect to new acquisitions. Throughout 1927 A. P. bought additional banks, not only in the San Francisco area, but in southern California's Orange County. He sought out sparsely populated localities in the eastern and northern counties of the state, especially in mining towns and timber communities near the Sierras. With these expanded holdings he undertook another consolidation on December 28, 1928, which also involved a significant change of name. Under this new reorganization the Bank of Italy was rechristened as the Bank of America. With 138 branches and $358 million in deposits, it became the second-largest state-chartered bank in the United States.

A. P. sincerely hoped that this merger might set the stage for transcontinental banking. He had first dreamed of such a possibility in 1912, when its achievement seemed unrealistic. Then in 1919 he had bought the East River National Bank in New York City. Although small, it could serve as an anchor for a coast-to-coast system. That bank had also acquired the Banca d'America e d'Italia in Italy, which had branches of its own. By 1924 he crystallized his ideas further, as was evident from a newspaper interview he gave in that year in which he declared:

> Under nationwide branch banking, an enterprise located in either the big city or the small village would have potential reservoirs of credit— perhaps running into hundreds of millions. Big business could do business anywhere. More: this borrowing power would be absolutely independent of local conditions.

The explanation, of course, is found in the word *diversification*. . . .
Why has California been an ideal proving ground for branch banking?
Because its productive resources are remarkably diversified. But we do
not present California as being so fully diversified as the entire United
States. Hence a nationwide system has far more assurance of success
from the very outset than had our statewide system.

During 1925 A. P. bought another bank in New York City, the
Bowery National Bank, and established twelve new branches in the
city. Consequently, by 1928 he was far closer to his grandiose goal.
As President Bacigalupi noted:

> Our unusual success has [not] been due to any superior knowledge or
> ability on our part . . . but we are convinced that the key to our success
> is to be found . . . in the economic, social, and political soundness of
> branch banking itself.
>   It is indeed difficult to understand why banks and their customers
> should be denied the efficiencies of large-scale "production" of nation-
> wide scope.
>   In our humble opinion this nation-wide development should be
> patterned after the structure of the Federal Reserve, rather than the
> English or Canadian systems. The establishment of nation-wide
> banks—owned and controlled by the people of the country—dividing
> their responsibilities and operations into twelve regional districts . . .
> dependent only upon a grand Central Head Office for general major
> policies . . . does not seem unworkable or improbable, and we make
> bold to hope that the day may soon arrive when such banks will be
> given legal approbation.

But economic conditions in the United States and around the world
as well as other problems soon were to dash these ambitious hopes.

A.P.'s mother, Virginia Scatena. *Bank of America Archives*

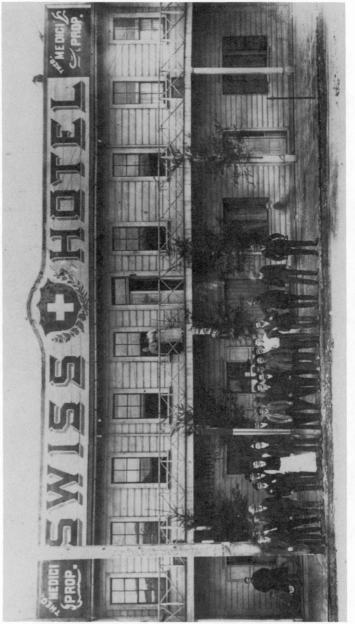

A.P.'s birthplace: the Swiss Hotel in San Jose, California. *Bank of America Archives*

A. P. and his bride, Clorinda Cuneo, 1892. *Bank of America Archives*

G.B. LEVAGGI

L. SCATENA

G. IACCHERI

CHAS. F. GRONDONA

A.P. GIANNINI

JAS. J. FAGAN

JOS. F. CAVAGNARO

ANT. CHICHIZOLA

GEO. G. CAGLIERI

First
Board of Directors
Bank of Italy
Incorporated 1904

G. COSTA

L. DEMARTINI

A. P. and the first board of directors of the Bank of Italy, 1904. *Bancroft Library*

A. P. and child movie star Jackie Coogan at the opening of Bank of America's Los Angeles headquarters, 1923. *Bank of America Archives*

A. P., banker incarnate, 1929. *Bank of America Archives*

ARTHUR REYNOLDS   DWIGHT L. CLARKE   Dr. A.H. GIANNINI   WARNERS EDMUNDS   A.P. GIANNINI

A. P., his brother A. H., and associates, 1930. *Bank of America Archives*

Fighting the depression: A. P. delivering the message during his "Back to the Good Times" campaign, 1932. *Bank of America Archives*

A. P. (*standing*) watching his son Mario as he assumed office as president of the Bank of America in 1936. *Bank of America Archives*

A. P. (*standing*) and California Governor Culbert L. Olson, 1941. *Bancroft Library*

The proud grandfather: A. P. with Anne Giannini (McWilliams) and her sister, Virginia Giannini (Hammerness), in 1947. *Bancroft Library*

A. P. as the head of the world's biggest bank in 1946. *Bank of America Archives*

A. P. in retirement: a formal portrait. *Bancroft Library*

CHAPTER 4

Management of the Empire, 1919–1927

THROUGHOUT the 1920s A. P. revealed extraordinary skills not only as an enterpriser but also as a manager. While he was building his increasingly complex system of banking institutions, he was also developing an organizational framework and a managerial style. In many ways he was as creative in administration as he was in his acquisitions, if also as determined and ruthless. If at times his banks in the 1920s reflected loose administration, that was often due to the speed with which he added new units to the system. By the end of the decade, however, as the outlines of the integrated empire took shape, he overcame many of the managerial problems and created a smoothly run, efficient operation.

Waxing philosophical in 1924, A. P. reflected on his managerial style. "It's no trick to run any business if a man has the intelligence and industry to concentrate on the job. The great trouble with most men is that they scatter too much. A few men can go into many things and succeed, but they are very few." Taking his own advice, he resigned his presidency of the bank in 1924 but remained as chairman of the executive committee. "I merely want to be free to concentrate on major policies," he said. "My boys are coming along satisfactorily, and I get a great satisfaction out of seeing their development."

Without question, A. P. was a rather authoritarian taskmaster. He had rather set ideas about people whom he hired as employees. For example, he himself worried little, he noted, because he concentrated all of his attention on the banking business. Thus, he had no use for individuals who were inclined to do otherwise. "We don't want on our staff anybody who worries," he said. If any of his employees showed evidence of spending time in worry over domestic problems, he was inclined to fire them. "If a man gets into debt, we don't want him either," he declared. "He'll worry." The mere presence of any of his employees in a gambling house was sufficient cause for dismissal.

He even disliked his son's Saturday night poker games in his San Mateo home, for he believed that bankers should project a conservative image, never one that would suggest even a hint of speculation.

For A. P. the banking business was not merely a road to wealth but represented a means of personal fulfillment, a world of excitement and infinite challenge. As one of his interviewers remarked in 1924: "The thing that Mr. Giannini is proudest of is the fact that he is a poor man. He has a salary, yes. It's a pretty good salary. But his tastes are simple. . . . 'When I die,' said Mr. Giannini, 'the world is going to be surprised at the little estate that I have left. It won't be a million. I have no sympathy for the man who just lives to make money. There may be pleasure in the game for some, but how futile.' "

Although a believer in decentralizing administrative operations of his bank, A. P. believed strongly in the concentration of control at the top. In view of that policy he consistently promoted a wide dissemination of stock ownership so that there would be few challenges to his decision making and control. In 1924, there were 13,692 individuals holding shares in the Bank of Italy, most of them owning 10 shares or less. Only 28 individuals held 350 or more shares each. A. P. himself owned 23,364 shares of a total of 175,000, making him the largest single stockholder. His determination was well reflected in a letter he wrote in 1918, when he was seeking to raise money to buy a New York bank. As he wrote to his negotiator: "Has anyone informed you that before I left there $1,500,000 had been subscribed by nine New York Italians? I do not want the big subscribers. It is my intention to have a campaign made among all the Italians there, with a view to interesting a couple of hundred of them. It was understood, at the time this $1,500,000 was subscribed, that a subscription list would be circulated among a couple thousand of the best Italian merchants of New York with the hope of having them sign up in sums of from $2,000–10,000 each."

In the following year he made his intentions even clearer. In the effort to round up new stockholders, he instructed his representative, James Bacigalupi, "Don't forget to point out what an Italian institution properly organized can do for the upbuilding, development, and prosperity of the Italian businessmen—particularly small ones." The leaders of New York's Italian business community were hardly inclined to share power either with A. P. or with large numbers of small investors. "The scheme is to keep control themselves," Bacigalupi wired his boss, "to use your name and reputation . . . and after a few years . . . to oust you." A. P. nipped their efforts in the bud, however, and began a large-scale recruitment drive of small investors with his own staff. "It is my desire to sell the stock in blocks of from five to one hundred shares each among all the Italians there," he informed his lieutenants. They were to recruit men whom Italians would respect. "There is no better medium to get to the people than through the priests and doctors," A. P. advised. "Tell Father Piperni that it is very likely that an Italian institution will be started there, which will mean the bringing together of the Italian people . . . and that it would be a good thing for all of the Italian priests to assist the proposed project in any way possible."

Although by 1924 the bank had grown to be a large institution, with several thousand employees, A. P. still believed in having trusted family members and close friends in key positions. He was especially proud of his son Mario. Since childhood Mario had been a hemophiliac. His affliction kept him awake nights and often interfered with his working days. Nevertheless, Mario was ambitious and began work for the bank while he was still in high school. After attending the University of California in Berkeley and graduating from its law school in 1920, he joined the bank on a full-time basis. For a while he worked in various branches and then transferred to the main office. By 1922 A. P. felt that his son was ready for a seat on the board of directors. Then he sent him to Italy for six months to gain international experience at the Bank of America there. On his return A. P. made him assistant to the president. "Relatives have to work harder than anyone around here to make good," his father told him early in his career.

Although he had a lifelong antagonistic relationship with his brother Attilio, A. P. gave him a key role in the bank as well. The two simply could not stand each other. In addition to strong personality conflicts, they also resented each other's backgrounds. While A. P. as a teenager had pounded the pavements of the waterfront to solicit business, Attilio had attended college at the University of California, where he also won athletic honors. He went on to medical school and served with some glory to himself as a medical officer in the Spanish-American War. In addition to building a successful medical practice in San Francisco during the next decade, he also served for four years on that city's board of supervisors.

Attilio throughout his life reminded his brother of what he considered to be his superiority. Even in 1936, when both were in their sixties, Attilio wrote A. P. that he had trouble comprehending one of his recent letters in garbled English. Resentfully A. P. shot back: "You have to admit, Doc, that I haven't had the educational advantages that you have had. You were born several years after me, and during those years, I worked very hard (getting up at midnight and in the early hours of the morning) to do my part toward laying the foundation that made those advantages possible for you." In 1909 Attilio married the daughter of a wealthy Los Angeles real estate developer and expanded on his expensive tastes. He frequented the best clubs and was usually impeccably dressed in dark suits. While A. P. was gregarious and direct, Attilio was distant, disdainful, and aloof. A. P. considered him vain, overly sensitive, and unappreciative. In turn, Attilio found his brother overbearing, authoritarian, insensitive, and crude.

The two could hardly be in the same room for five minutes without acrimonious argument. And A. P.'s one-upmanship in relation to his brother was legendary. Attilio came to manage most of the bank's operations in southern California and, for a while, New York City. His business acumen was considerable, and he was a significant factor in the bank's growth.

A. P. also proved himself to be extraordinarily adept in adapting banking functions to the special needs of the western economy. Diversification of California agriculture had progressed so far by the 1920s that a flexible banking system invited success. At the same time, the rapid expansion of population in the state, especially in urban areas of the south and in Los Angeles, opened up vast new profitable markets. Other bankers were also well aware of these developments, but A. P. was particularly skillful in utilizing them to profit his own institution.

A case in point was his use of bankers' acceptances to expand available credit. These were drafts that came with the guarantee of a signer's bank that the local Federal Reserve Bank accepted. Their use allowed the Bank of Italy greatly to enlarge its lending capacity. As the *San Francisco Bulletin* commented on A. P.'s manipulation of this technique: "California has been hitched to a star. That star is the Federal Reserve Board. The Bank of Italy did the hitching. . . . A new financial harness has been fitted for the first time on this Coast. . . . Heretofore, the crops have been moved with the assistance of straight bank loans." By the use of such devices A. P. was able to cushion credit crises of major farm groups such as the California

Apricot and Prune Growers Association or the California Bean Growers Association. His policies demonstrated that small local banks in particular areas could not muster the increasingly large financial resources needed to tide over their local or the statewide growers. The increasingly sizable credit needs of large-scale commercial operations necessitated banks with vast resources who could shift their capital during particular seasons or to particular crops as needed during different times of the year. By the 1920s fully one-half of all the funds loaned by the Bank of Italy served the needs of agribusiness in the state.

A. P. was also skilled in utilizing federal programs to expand his bank's operations. One of these was long-term loans for capital improvements at low interest rates available under the Federal Farm Loan Act of 1916. The act allowed the establishment of privately owned but federally controlled joint stock land banks. A. P. in 1919 was one of the first in California to organize such a bank, which also allowed him to operate similar institutions in Oregon, Idaho, and Utah.

A. P.'s bank policies were tinged with conservatism and caution. Unlike other institutions, his was able to weather a succession of farm crises without serious losses and to establish itself as the dominant purveyor of farm credit in California during the 1920s. Innovative as A. P. was in so many ways, he was also a deep-dyed conservative in many others. He was always especially careful in his appraisal of real estate used as collateral for loans, and his caution permeated his entire banking system. As a rule, his bank's loans tended to be for one-third of the valuation of a particular parcel of real estate. Quite often, however, the bank's appraisals of real property were for only one-tenth of current market value.

A. P. also established special subsidiaries to cater to newly emerging industries. Cotton was a case in point. World War I did much to stimulate the development of large-scale cotton culture in California. Yet A. P. was extremely cautious in his initial financing of the thousands of new producers who now began to grow cotton. Once the industry was reasonably well established, however, he entered in a big way after 1924, financing producers, processors, and manufacturers. By 1929 his bank was financing fully one-half of the state's cotton crop, as California came to challenge Mississippi as the nation's biggest producer.

Among A. P.'s most imaginative financing in the period between the world wars was the motion picture industry. In this sphere he often relied on his brother, Attilio, who as early as 1909 began to extend small loans to pioneers in this field. In that year Attilio lent $500 to one Sol L. Lesser, who was a partner in a nickelodeon on Fillmore Street in San Francisco. Seven years later Lesser was head of All Features Distributors, a major firm. He continued to conduct most of his bank business with the Bank of Italy.

When Attilio moved to New York City in 1919 to manage the East River National Bank, he did not give up his interest in the motion picture industry. In fact, he authorized an increasingly larger volume of credit to Hollywood enterprises, including Mack Sennett and Vitagraph. He also helped the Schenck Brothers, who got their start with movie houses south of Fourteenth Street in New York City, not far from Giannini's East River Bank on Broadway. Within a few years they built a studio across the Hudson River on the New Jersey Palisades.

Attilio made it his business to know most of the pioneers in the movie business and built an extensive network of contacts in the industry. By 1921 more than twenty-five distributing companies were circulating films to about sixteen thousand theaters in the United States, and most of the major firms had accounts with the Bank of Italy. The Lessers, for example, passed on the news about the bank's willingness to lend to some of their friends, such as Louis Selznick, Marcus Loew, and a host of others who shortly were to become moguls in the industry. Biograph, General Films, Vitagraph, and Lubin were in the Bank of Italy fold. Giannini's largest advance during this period was $250,000 to First National Distributors for the production of Charles Chaplin's hit *The Kid*. Such was the success of this picture that the company repaid the loan within six weeks after it had first shown the film. As Attilio noted in 1926: "If a film is offered me starring Doug [Fairbanks], Charlie [Chaplin], Harold [Lloyd], or any of a half dozen leading actors, it is as good as cash. Where I am in doubt, I call up any of a half-dozen theater managers and get an immediate rating."

After 1923 the bank became even more closely identified with the motion picture industry. A. P. named Joseph M. Schenck and Cecil B. DeMille to the advisory board of one of the bank's branches in Los Angeles. Will Rogers, Conrad Nagel, and Sol Lesser soon served in similar capacities. DeMille actually became president of the Commercial and Savings Bank of Culver City, a Giannini subsidiary in the

Los Angeles area. Through such individuals A. P. became intimately acquainted with the special needs of this fledgling industry. Unlike traditional bankers, he began to accept motion picture rights to innovative plays or books as security for loans and considered assignment of box office receipts as well. At the same time, he charged lower interest rates than financiers, who were still rather suspicious about the economic soundness of motion pictures.

Once in a while A. P. had anxious moments with his motion picture friends. In 1924 A. P. was presiding over a director's meeting at the Commercial National Bank of Los Angeles to celebrate the release of DeMille's *Ten Commandments*. DeMille was not only an old friend of A. P. but at the time was also serving as vice-president of the Cherokee Avenue branch of the Bank of Italy. DeMille seemed nervous but said little. As he later told the story, he had lent $200,000 to Sam Goldwyn without authorization from the head office, as regulations required. After A. P. went back to San Francisco, DeMille began to worry but hesitated to call him on the phone. Instead, he chartered a plane and flew to San Francisco to present the news in person. As he walked through the doors of the still-rather-new headquarters at One Powell Street, A. P. noticed him and provided a personal tour of the building. After an hour of banter DeMille finally broke the news. A. P. was somewhat nonplussed and requested future notice of such large loans. DeMille stressed that he was more than a figurehead, however, and that his presence at the Bank of Italy brought in a good deal of new business. Finally the two titans parted amiably. DeMille retained his affiliation with the bank, while A. P. rarely missed a DeMille opening.

Yet it must be said that it was Attilio rather than A. P. who deserved primary credit for developing the bank's relations with the motion picture industry. Attilio was sympathetic to many of the fledgling movie producers who were of immigrant background just like the Gianninis. Most of the older established bankers shunned these people. "We stepped in to make loans to deserving companies," Attilio noted. "Our loans were at the current rate of interest. I simply decided that motion pictures were good merchandise, as good as cotton, wheat, or barley." Attilio also solicited bank deposits from movie people and sold them bank stock. Norma Talmadge, a leading movie star who was also the wife of Joseph Schenck, was among the biggest depositors. Others who served as directors or stockholders included Charlie Chaplin, Will Rogers, Wallace Beery, Mary Pickford, and

Douglas Fairbanks, Sr. In turn, Attilio was a director of many movie studios. He was on the board of Columbia Pictures and settled many a conflict between owners Harry and Jack Cohn. He delighted in arranging screen tests for budding actors and actresses. And he helped studio executives like Jack Warner with his severe gambling and drinking problems. As one Hollywood gossiper noted: "The Doc's been more than a banker to Hollywood. Everyone in Hollywood cried on his shoulders." Attilio was convinced that his brother was not appreciative of his efforts. "We have a monopoly of the picture business," Attilio wrote A. P. with some exaggeration. "I think that is some record." But if he used his customary hyperbole, it was true that during the 1920s the bank extended more than $100 million in loans to theater owners and producers.

In many ways the Bank of Italy as it developed in the 1920s was an extension of A. P.'s personality. During the decade it more than kept pace with California's burgeoning population and the more than two million newcomers. Yet A. P.'s personality pervaded many of its operations, including his motto, "Safety before profit." Although the bank moved extensively into real estate, it refrained from extensive involvement with large-scale developers and subdividers, or financing of hotels and apartment buildings. Instead, A. P. stuck by his policy of seeking out small home buyers or small store owners, who were less likely to be involved in speculative schemes. Although California underwent an oil boom in the 1920s, A. P. mostly refrained from involvement in that industry, which he considered highly speculative. Subsequent events during the Great Depression confirmed his judgment. In contrast, he felt that the motion picture industry presented great opportunities for his institution and so made his bank the preeminent financier of Hollywood ventures. At the same time, he consolidated his role as the major purveyor of capital to the state's booming agribusiness. In the 1920s, therefore, expansion in home and small-business loans and in the growing consumer market in appliances and automobiles, agribusiness, and motion pictures provided major building blocks for the bank's growth, directly reflecting A. P.'s judgment on sound economic development.

Yet A. P. could not have built the banking empire that he did if it had not been for his distinctive style of management. In the 1920s he institutionalized many of the methods and policies that had contributed to his success in earlier years. Thus he maintained an effective mix between centralization at headquarters and decentralization in subregions and branches. This affected even the physical appearance of his branches as well as the personnel with which he staffed them. He favored wide dissemination of stock ownership, both in different communities and in his own organization, since employees were encouraged to buy shares. He continued the practice of having leading citizens serve on advisory boards of his branch banks, involving them in a variety of ways. He continued intensive advertising of his services and direct solicitation. While appealing to people in a mass market, he was keenly aware of the psychological barriers banks sometimes erected for customers with modest means. His banks tried to avoid such obstacles and therefore contained few closed offices, no barred teller cages; they were designed to be open, inviting, and, above all, informal. Unlike his competitors, he made special appeals to racial and ethnic minorities and indeed created special divisions to solicit their business.

In fact, these special divisions were a unique feature of the Bank of Italy. Other banks usually ignored minorities, in part because of language barriers. For their part, immigrants tended to be timid or suspicious about using banks in their adopted land. A. P. well understood this emotional response and made an effective place for himself as an intermediary and trusted consultant. Immigrants usually generated more bank business than the native born, since they habitually sent money back to their native countries. San Francisco had always had its share of foreign banks to serve this trade. They included the German Savings Bank and Loan Society, the Swiss Italian-American Bank, the Portuguese-American Bank, the French-American Bank, and the Sumimoto Bank. A. P. competed with these institutions on his home grounds but was innovative in extending such activities even into remote areas of California. Eventually the business extension department came to supervise separate ethnic divisions of the bank, including Greek, Russian, Slavonian, Portuguese, Latin-American, Spanish, and Chinese divisions. The largest was the Italian department, which continued to send out scores of solicitors each year. Each division employed individuals who were fluent in the language and knowledgeable in the culture of a particular group. In this decade at least 20 percent of the depositors were Italian, although more than twice as many were stockholders. Other divisions were smaller but significant. The Chinese section, under Nelson N. Yue, gained several thousand new accounts each year. The Greek division catered to about five thousand in the bay area, while the number of

Portuguese, Russians, and Slavonians numbered more than thirty thousand.

To tie these and other groups even more closely to the bank, A. P. created a business advisory service. It provided advice and guidance for a wide range of small-business enterprises. On any given day his branches counted among their customers butchers, bakers, peddlers, janitors, marble cutters, rag pickers, loggers, fishermen, farmers, viti-culturists, to name only a few. No one was too insignificant or unimportant to be ignored, and his sales force hunted all. And A. P. insisted that all be given courteous treatment.

It was A. P.'s personal belief that the architecture of his banks should be kept simple. He surmised quite correctly that the marble palaces the banks had been accustomed to building exuded an aura of extravagance that tended to intimidate clients of modest means. Most of his branches during these years were simple, square, or oblong structures with a utilitarian bent. The interior consisted of teller's stations along both walls, interspersed by open spaces where he placed the desks of managers and customer agents—usually as close to the entrance doors as possible. In a time when most banks put their tellers behind grilled cages and their officers in private suites with locked doors, A. P. practiced openness. His officers had no private spaces but sat accessible at desks behind low railings near the front doors. His tellers mostly were not separated from customers by iron grills, often not even by partitions. Not all branches were identi-cal, of course. In wealthy neighborhoods or in his headquarters at Montgomery Street, his buildings reflected much greater opulence and a more formal decor, as was expected by his clients.

A variety of reasons motivated A. P. to favor a wide dissemination of his bank's stock. Such a policy allowed him to exercise prime control and to fend off challenges to his power. At the same time, it reflected his business philosophy in attracting a mass rather than a class market. The policy had other advantages as well. It bred a feeling of loyalty and a sense of community among tens of thousands of his small depositors, who viewed their branches as small neighborhood banks rather than as units of one of the nation's banking giants. There they could see familiar faces in an informal and unintimidating atmosphere. And each branch had an advisory board composed of leading men and women in the community who were well known locally and enjoyed the respect and trust of their fellow citizens. Most average citizens understood little about banking but identified their bank with people and faces they could trust. A. P. understood this factor so much better than did most of his fellow bankers. The concept also reflected A. P.'s own personality, that of a gregarious, hand-shaking individual who was genuinely interested in other people, whether rich or poor. In every community scores of individuals owned a few shares of stock in the bank or knew some member of the advisory board. They felt a personal stake in the institution and had a feeling of loyalty few other banks could match. And although A. P. was often accused of being an autocrat, in his perspective the bank personified democracy at work.

Irrespective of the offices he held, A. P. was the dominant power figure in the bank during the 1920s. To assist him he selected a proven group of managers, who remained loyal to him. Few of the original founders of the bank were still active in the 1920s, but they included his father, Pop Scatena, who served as chairman of the board, and Vice-President Armando Pedrini, one of his first employees. His brother George, who headed Scatena and Company, the fruit commission firm that A. P. had helped to build, served as a bank director. Another key associate was Prentice Cobb Hale, a scion of one of California's prominent merchant families. A. P. had first met Hale when he secured his first branch in 1911 in San Jose, where Hale operated one of his department stores. A white-haired and distinguished-looking merchant of old Yankee lineage, Hale provided A. P. with an entrée on his bank-buying expeditions that A. P.—a man of Italian-American immigrant background, with a foreign sounding name, and of Catholic religion—could not have secured by himself. Hale proved crucial to A. P.'s bank purchases for almost two decades.

A. P. was also adept in coopting talented bankers into his own organization. Some, like William A. Williams, were former California state bank superintendents. Others were prominent bankers such as Harry C. Carr, former president of the California League of Independent Bankers. He had been president of his own bank in Porterville when A. P. bought it, and then A. P. made him vice-president of the Bank of Italy in charge of country branches. Many other officers of banks that A. P. absorbed had similar experiences and continued productive careers in the Bank of Italy system.

By 1929 A. P. had built one of the largest banking empires in the United States. He accomplished this feat in a little more than two decades. Without question, a favorable economic environment in California provided him with a crucible for his extraordinary accomplishments. But in addition, his special talents contributed to his rise. He was not only a remarkable enterpriser but an effective manager. This dual combination made him a major force in American banking. But A. P. had been able to take advantage of an expansive business climate in most phases of his long career. Whether he could be successful in the midst of adverse economic conditions such as those ushered in by the Great Crash of 1929 was an open question. The depression was to test A. P.'s mettle.

CHAPTER 5

A. P. and the Great Depression, 1927–1940

BY 1927 A. P.'s dreams had grown more expansive, for now he envisaged a nationwide banking system extending from coast to coast. Having established a statewide and limited regional chain of branch banks in the West, he hoped to expand these across the nation and then perhaps to grow on a global scale. That would provide a crowning achievement to a truly spectacular career.

But until 1927 A. P. had built his banking empire within the context of statewide, regional, and countrywide prosperity. In fact, much of his success had lain in his uncanny and extraordinary ability to discern contemporary and future economic trends—to anticipate them, to exploit them, and, in some cases, to create them. In part his genius lay in his ability to adapt his banking operations to the special dynamics of California's economy and that of the West. In these efforts he had been brilliantly successful and had outgunned many of his competitors. Between 1927 and 1940, however, he found himself in a very different economic environment. For the moment, economic expansion ceased, in California as elsewhere, and after 1929 the worst depression conditions in the nation's history challenged the ingenuity of even the most experienced bankers. The favorable conditions in which he had found himself during much of his life were gone. Instead, he faced a much more difficult economic environment in which survival and consolidation presented far greater challenges than the expansion of branch banking. Such times obviously required managerial skills of a different order, skills different from those he had developed in his earlier years. Or so it seemed. It was a tribute to A. P.'s talents that he rose to the challenges of the Great Depression and preserved his banking empire intact amid crises and tribulations.

The depression clearly affected A. P.'s plans to establish a transcontinental banking system. As the economy faltered, his lifelong dream seemed to evaporate. Nor was he even able to complete the building of a comprehensive network of branch banks in his native West.

Those hopes had to be shelved for the moment. Instead, he had to address the pressing problems created by the economic crisis. These included the loss of his banking empire and a bitter fight to regain control. This conflict absorbed most of his energies from 1930 to 1932. Then he faced problems of solvency such as he had rarely confronted in the past. As in earlier years, he found it expedient to become involved in politics to further his bank's objectives. Until 1937 he was an avid supporter of the New Deal.

A. P. took pressure well. During these difficult years he reflected much of the same flexibility that had resulted in his earlier successes, by resorting to the imaginative adaptation of new business methods that helped to sustain his institutions during the uncertain period. Between 1937 and 1940 he could breathe more easily because he had ensured its survival, but he had made important enemies along the way who threatened to block his larger plans for expansion in the future. Nevertheless, as captain of the ship between 1927 and 1940 (his son Mario actually held the official titles in the bank and directed daily administration), A. P. proved himself able to steer a clear course through weather more foul than fair, although he had to brave violent storms along the way.

Fresh from his triumph with the passage of the McFadden Act of 1927, A. P. looked to the establishment of a nationwide system of branch banks coast to coast. His vision was far ahead of that of other bankers of his day; the practices he envisaged developed only after the 1980s. Consequently he encountered obstacles that prevented him from fulfilling his dream. Worsening economic conditions obviously made the effort more difficult, but other impediments also blocked his path. Increasingly he faced opposition from eastern bankers, especially J. P. Morgan, Jr. The unexpected manipulation of Bank of America stock by speculators proved to be another roadblock. And his faulty judgment in selecting his successor created further difficulties.

A. P.'s interest in branch banking had developed over the years. Already in 1912, it will be remembered, he had traveled to New York City to discuss the opening of a branch with leaders of the Italian community. That proposal did not materialize because A. P. was unwilling to leave California to manage the unit, as the New Yorkers desired. In 1919 he did purchase the East River National Bank, however, which gave him an outlet in New York. To hold the stock of this new institution he created the Bancitaly, a holding company that also held stock of some of his banks in Italy and in San Francisco. By the mid-1920s A. P. was using it as an instrument to bypass the state bank superintendent or the U.S. comptroller whenever they denied him permits for new branches. But A. P. decided that to spearhead his drive for national prominence he really needed to purchase a major, and hopefully prestigious, New York bank. In the spring of 1928 he journeyed to New York City on such a shopping expedition, determined to acquire a bastion within the Wall Street establishment.

But the eastern bankers were wary of this brash newcomer from California, an immigrant's son, with an Italian name to boot. Their conceptions of banking also clashed directly with those of A. P. His broad goal was to tap the mass markets composed of millions of small depositors and lenders. Theirs was to deal with a class market consisting of upper-class people of wealth. And while A. P. was impatient to get on with the creation of a nationwide network of branch banks, Morgan was not about to let the upstart from California assume the lead. Moreover, A. P. indicated that whatever bank he bought should have "S. A." (Savings Association) added to its title because it would "serve to advertise to the people of New York that strong institutions are now doing a savings business." But the New York bankers looked upon small savings accounts with contempt and objected to his suggestions.

Although he hoped to be accepted as a member of the Wall Street "club," A. P. was not overly subtle and infuriated them further, especially Morgan. A. P.'s agent, Leo Belden, had been scouting the New York banking scene in 1928, looking for a prestigious bank A. P. might acquire. He thought that he had found just the right institution to serve as anchor, the Bank of America at 44 Wall Street. Founded in 1812, it was one of the city's oldest financial bastions. Not only did it have a sterling reputation, but it also boasted a very profitable trust department and close connections to the House of Morgan. To attempt the purchase, however, A. P. was forced to ask for Morgan's permission. As events were to turn out, that was a fatal miscalculation on A. P.'s part. Initially, it is true, Morgan seemed friendly, if rather cool. He first met A. P. at the home of one of the Morgan associates on March 9, 1928. "A. P. was informed," reported a participant in the meeting, "that his acquiring control of the Bank of America would . . . have the blessing of J. P. Morgan and Co." Mario Giannini noted at the time that he believed "Morgan chose us . . . because he felt he could dictate." In any event, A. P. concluded the transaction in March of 1928. He bought a majority of shares in the Bank of America for

$17 million and merged it with his smaller East River National Bank
to form what he hoped would be a new major anchor—the Bank of
America N.T. and Savings Association.

But almost immediately Morgan made other demands. Nor were
he and his associates above heaping small humiliations on this band
of Italian-Americans who were invading what had been until then
largely a Yankee bastion. The eastern bankers were determined to
make life difficult for the unorthodox westerners. Thus Morgan insisted that A. P. deposit at least $1 million in a Morgan bank, in
addition to deposits that had already been agreed upon. A. P. grum-
bled but bit his tongue and complied. Morgan was also incensed that
A. P. broke a New York banking tradition by reducing the price of
Bank of America's capital stock to $25 per share so as to allow broad
distribution, when the accepted minimum in the fraternity had long
been $100 per share. The New York banker also played the dominant
role in selecting a new board of directors, most of whom were
prestigious New Yorkers representing the Wall Street establishment.
A. P. was terribly dismayed when he found that only a very few
Italian-Americans were given places. The Wall Streeters relegated
most of A. P.'s ethnic associates to an obscure advisory board. Although A. P.'s brother Attilio was nominally chairman of the board,
he was highly insulted when at the first meeting of the directors
Morgan's representatives tried to prevent him from presiding. To
add further insult to injury, they did not provide him with suitable
executive office space and frequently made loud, uncomplimentary
remarks about Italian-Americans. And such was Morgan's influence
with top officials at the Federal Reserve Bank of New York that they
required A. P. to convert Bancitaly stock to individual ownership to
operate as a trust company, rather than as a holding operation. A. P.
had no choice but to comply. Unfortunately for him, this created a
new sea of troubles because now he could exercise very little control
over speculation in the bank's stock.

In fact, wild speculation in Bank of America shares during 1928
and 1929 seriously impeded A. P.'s plans for nationwide banking.
Even in April and May 1928, just after he had acquired the bank and
left for a vacation in Europe, the swing of his bank's stocks was
violent. A. P. became alarmed. "Stock selling too high. Discourage
purchase," he cabled his associate James Bacigalupi on April 12, 1928,
from his vacation spa. In June, Bank of America stock plunged while
A. P. lay ill with pleurisy in a Rome hotel. The price decline weakened

him financially and lessened his stature even more in the eyes of the eastern bankers. He returned to the United States in September, determined to avoid such embarrassments in the future. For that purpose he created still another holding company for all of his banks, the Transamerica Corporation. On January 1, 1929, this new entity became a reality while A. P. made sure that it had a majority of Californians on its board of directors.

This action only worsened the tensions between A. P. and the Wall Street group. More and more they distrusted his style of banking and looked down their noses at him and his staff. "Ingratiating methods will never do with these fellows," Attilio complained to his brother. "For many years they have been impossible and must be told where to head in. . . . The gang downtown never cared for our kind, and never will. It is true we need them now, but [it] is not necessary to have them ride over us."

By late 1929 A. P. had concluded that further appeasement of Morgan would be unproductive and that he would simply have to meet him head on. To lessen the influence of the easterners, he now proposed to consolidate his new Transamerica Corporation further, a move opposed by Morgan, who threatened a complete break if A. P. went in that direction. A. P. pondered Morgan's demands awhile but decided he would have to risk his antagonism if he was to proceed with his plans for nationwide banking. And so he withdrew all of his funds from the Morgan banks and prepared to continue his New York operations without Morgan's help and approval. To direct his New York anchor he appointed an experienced and prestigious Wall Street banker, Elisha P. Walker, as chief executive of Transamerica Corporation.

Just as the Great Crash ushered in the depression, A. P.'s own health also hit bottom. His polyneuritis had gotten worse over the years and now was extremely painful. It had induced him to retire as chairman of Transamerica and to select Walker to take his place. A. P. now hoped to find some relief by visiting the German and Austrian spas that he had found soothing in the past. During the next two years he was in Europe undergoing therapeutic treatments, far removed from the bank's difficulties at home. However, since he had chosen his son Mario as president of Transamerica, he was in constant touch, sending streams of cables.

Unfortunately, the news became increasingly unfavorable as A. P.'s bank, like many others, plunged into turmoil. Initially Walker had intended to continue A. P.'s expansionist policies. But after the crash he took a closer look at Transamerica's books and was disturbed. The bank owned large blocks of stocks in major corporations whose value had depreciated significantly in the general decline of stock prices. Yet the bank's accountants continued to list their value at original purchase prices. By 1930 Walker felt he had no alternative but to write off more than $1 billion so that the books would reflect the true situation more accurately. Outside bank examiners also questioned the quality of a substantial portion of the bank's loans. That led Walker to oust a substantial number of employees in order to cut expenses. Worst of all, in A. P.'s opinion, was his decision to reduce and eventually to eliminate the bank's dividend. Reflecting his pessimism, Walker also announced publicly that the book value of Transamerica, pegged in 1929 at $49.82 per share, had declined to $14.50 per share two years later, and might drop still more. Although he merged the Bank of Italy (which now went out of existence) with the Bank of America in 1930 into one giant conglomerate, the Bank of America National Trust and Savings Association, Walker intended to sell its assets in order to keep the institution solvent and afloat.

These actions outraged the Gianninis. They openly challenged the gloomy evaluations of the company's financial condition by outside accountants. They opposed reductions of the dividend. They wanted to fight the stock speculators who continued to drive down the bank's share prices. Walker's reaction was to treat the Gianninis with contempt. When in January 1931 he let Mario (who was president) cool his heels for several hours in the anteroom to his office, where he consulted with a stream of other bank officers, Mario could stand it no longer. He resigned as president and poured out his anger in a stream of telegrams to his father. The very thought of dismemberment of the empire that had taken him a lifetime to build infuriated A. P. In June of 1931 he spent thousands of dollars to send cables to Walker by the score, hoping to dissuade him from his policy of paring down the bank. But Walker would not budge. On June 20, 1931, A. P. therefore resigned as chairman of the advisory committee of Transamerica so that he could fight more vehemently. In emotional tones he commented that "as the New Yorkers have it, I am only a peddler, and a lowly one at that. Perhaps they are right . . . [but] the plan to sell [assets] is a deliberate steal."

In September 1931 A. P.'s health was still precarious, but he was itching to begin a battle to regain control over his beloved bank. As he wrote to Mario, he was "waiting only to recover health and strength to give the dirty gang a real stiff battle when the right moment to strike arrives." Hoping to remain incognito, he began the long journey home to surprise his enemies. On September 22, 1931, he appeared at Transamerica's board meeting, where he presented his views opposing the various Walker policies. Facing a hostile board, he was consistently outvoted, since Walker had complete control.

A. P. was not dissuaded. Strangely enough, the prospect of a bitter battle did wonders for his health. The conflict was to have a far greater therapeutic effect than years of therapy in Europe. To the amazement of his doctors, in the next few months he rapidly regained full strength. Late in 1931 he began a major campaign to rally Transamerica's 200,000 stockholders to his side and to vote the Walker team out of office at the next corporate election, which was planned for February 1932.

Many of his former associates were dubious about his prospects, also reflecting the pessimism of the depression years. Meanwhile, eastern bankers gloated. They had a majority of directors at Transamerica and most had close ties to Morgan or the old Boston house of Lee, Higginson and Company, another banking conglomerate friendly to Morgan. As the *American Banker* noted at the time:

> A meteor in the banking firmament disintegrates with A. P. Giannini's loss of control of Transamerica Corporation and its far flung affiliates. Viewing the results, the majority of bankwise and financially minded observers abroad as well as at home, will be likely to breathe easier. . . . Giannini overshot the mark. The shortening of his shadow in the banking world will be good for banking in a future that should look askance at too large financial egg-baskets.

A. P. saw it differently, however. "Ours was an institution with soul," he lamented, "and working solely for the interests of stockholders [of modest means]." Critics might scoff, but such was the vision that fired his energies as he went off to battle.

His immediate goal was to orchestrate a massive campaign—much like a political contest—to win a majority of votes from the 200,000 Transamerica stockholders. Up and down California he went, speaking to shareholders at meetings, where often thousands appeared. They shook his hands, asked questions, and were usually well impressed. He also visited local branches, greeted customers and employees, kissed babies, and cultivated a positive image. The battle was between

California and Wall Street, he declared. A typical meeting was one in Stockton, California, where four thousand people crowded into the Civic Auditorium to hear him and his representative, who declared:

> Do these two or three Wall Street bankers imagine we are a bunch of fools—200,000 California investors who will sit still in the face of a financial "cleanout" carry the economic and political control of California to two or three persons in New York? Do they think they can get away with Russian methods in giving orders to their employees that if they do not dissuade stockholders from joining our organization they will be fired?

The reference was to the stern policies of the Walker regime, which threatened to fire employees who were not active in the fight against Giannini, a potent demand in the depths of the depression, when jobs were scarce. As the campaign became more heated, A. P. hit his stride and seemed largely rejuvenated. When the votes were tallied on February 15, 1932, they revealed an overwhelming victory for him. He secured 15.3 million shares supporting his slate, compared with 9.5 million for Walker. A. P. once more assumed the position as chairman of the board, together with a group representing his supporters.

By 1932 A. P. was back at the helm of Transamerica. On February 23, 1932, he returned to the bank's headquarters at One Powell Street. He sat down at his old desk, in an open room without partitions, so that he could look at customers and staff. It seemed like old times. But for the moment the pressing problems of the depression forced him to shelve his ever-present goal of creating nationwide banking structures. His most immediate challenge was to save what was left of the Bank of America and to nurse it back to health.

Without losing much time, A. P. settled down to work with that same ferocious energy he had poured into building the bank in earlier years. First, he sought to win back some of his former large accounts who had drifted away during his absence. These included the Pacific Telephone and Telegraph Company, I. Magnin and Company, and F. W. Woolworth. Second, he hoped to win more small depositors. As in his youth, he prowled the streets of San Francisco's fruit and vegetable districts at 5:00 A.M. in the morning, shaking hands and sending his staff to solicit new accounts, ring doorbells, and drum up business for the bank. He and his associates also visited scores of the bank's branches, where they greeted customers and hoped to motivate and shake up the local staff. Third, he imposed drastic economies on the bank. In addition to substantial layoffs, he cut salaries of officers and employees and forced many to take involuntary furloughs.

Always aware of the importance of publicity and image, he launched a "Back to Good Times" campaign, utilizing radio spots, billboards, and direct mailings. A. P. appealed to Californians to replace fear with confidence in their state's future. "Keep your dollars moving," bank advertisements counseled, and "speed up the wheels of California's industry." On the bank's weekly radio program he told his listeners, "I can say with *real* conviction that I believe that the hysterical stage of the depression is past. I have confidence in the courage and resourcefulness of the American people. And I have unbounded faith in the people and resources of California. A movement such as ours can give the momentum so necessary to the complete restoration of public confidence and normal business conditions."

Finally, A. P. approached the new federal lending agency, the Reconstruction Finance Corporation, for loans to help tide his bank over the difficult period. His campaigns were infectious. Within the first few months he increased deposits by more than $50 million. He was not a miracle worker, however, and by October 1932 another wave of panic swept the nation and seriously affected most of its banks. It became clear that he would have to devote all of his energies simply to the preservation of the institution and that plans for expansion were irrelevant.

In this crisis he resorted to another technique that had often stood him in good stead—the use of political influence. As the presidential election of 1932 approached, both major candidates solicited his support, although A. P. was careful not to make formal endorsements. He let it be known in various informal ways, however, that he favored Roosevelt. Like many Americans, A. P. feared a total collapse of the economic system if the Hoover policies were continued. Moreover, he greatly resented appointments that Hoover made to the Reconstruction Finance Corporation. Some of them, like Eugene Meyer, A. P. considered to be his enemies in the banking profession, which illustrates his chronic streak of paranoia. Others, he was convinced, represented the Wall Street establishment. Although possibly exaggerated, his fears were not wholly unfounded. He was also angered by the agency's policy of publicizing loans it made to banks such as his own, without perhaps recognizing the public responsibilities of a government corporation. Without question, therefore, A. P. leaned toward FDR, and he so informed one of Roosevelt's backers, Joseph P. Kennedy, with whom he had engaged in many business dealings. In fact, A. P. told him that he would be glad to meet the candidate when the New Yorker campaigned in California. There Roosevelt delivered his memorable Commonwealth Club address in San Francisco, one of the few speeches in which he laid out broad lines of public policies. In the ensuing election FDR handily won California, much to A. P.'s pleasure. He looked forward hopefully to some improvement of the economy.

But the period of the four months between Roosevelt's election and his inauguration on March 4, 1933, witnessed some of the most critical months of the depression. As Hoover and Roosevelt were loath to discuss possible governmental action, the economic crisis deepened. Banks and financial institutions were especially affected as business failures and bankruptcies multiplied. By February 1933 the situation was so serious that the governors in two-thirds of the states ordered banks closed to save those that were still solvent.

A. P. was obviously affected by this growing crisis. As early as November 1932, when the Wingfield-Reno National Bank collapsed, the governor of Nevada appealed to A. P. to take over the institution as a salvage measure. A. P. agreed to do so, but with great reluctance. But by January 1933 the Nevada governor was forced to proclaim a state bank holiday. During the same month banks in southern California also closed their doors because they lacked funds demanded by their depositors. The strains on A. P.'s branches were enormous, and he was barely able to keep them open. Meanwhile, Roosevelt began consultations with leading bankers in the nation. He invited a select group, including A. P., to his town house in New York City, where on February 21 he listened to their views. A. P. also talked to various members of the new president's staff. Then, on February 23 A. P. met with Roosevelt and William H. Woodfin, designated by FDR as the new secretary of the treasury, and Jesse Jones, who was to be the incoming chairman of the Reconstruction Finance Corporation. The group made no major decisions. It was FDR's style to pick the brains of others before making up his own mind. On this occasion he was sounding out financiers about their general ideas concerning economic recovery. As A. P. reported the meeting to his son:

> Governor [Roosevelt] was very cordial. Jones is very friendly and boosted us to Governor. Governor is going to propose legislation take

care of farmers and home owners, issuing couple or three bonds in
place of present mortgages on a basis around sixty or seventy per cent
of face value. . . . Eugene [Meyer] is going to go in due course . . .
and there is likelihood of reorganization FRB [Federal Reserve
Board], with new memberships . . . in about five or six months.

A. P. applauded FDR's closing of the banks during the first week
of the new administration and much of the emergency legislation
during the One Hundred Days (March–June 1933). His support of
Roosevelt was to result in important dividends for the Bank of
America. The most important one was in the Emergency Banking
Act of 1933, which provided special advantages for the Bank of
America. "No other banking group gains from this act as many
advantages as does Transamerica," wrote A. P.'s chief lobbyist in
Washington, C. W. Collins, to his boss, reflecting on his own handi-
work with understandable enthusiasm.

Several sections of the act conferred benefits on A. P.'s system. Of
special value to A. P. was a provision that gave national banks the
same rights as state banks to open branches anywhere within a state
where state banks were allowed to do so. This enabled A. P. to merge
his Bank of America of California with his national banks, mainly the
Bank of America N.T. and S.A. Within a year this allowed him to
consolidate his 423 branches in 255 communities, leaving him with
only one state-chartered bank with eight branches. He deliberately
maintained that institution in case he wanted to switch back from a
national to a state-chartered system as he had done on previous
occasions. The act also allowed A. P. to open branches in states
outside of California. He put this provision to immediate use in
Oregon and Nevada. A third advantage stemmed from a proposal
A. P. had made in his testimony before the House Committee on
Banking and Currency, which had drafted the legislation. This provided for the extension of federal supervision over bank holding
companies like his Transamerica Corporation, a step that he viewed
as providing greater stability. A fourth provision that he influenced
was one that permitted minority stockholders in a national bank the
right to elect representatives to the board of directors in proportion
to the stock they held. This pertained directly to a problem he had
encountered with the National City Bank of New York. Transamerica
still owned 10 percent of its stock. But when A. P. bought it, J. P.
Morgan had insisted that he forgo representation on its board, or so
A. P. believed. At any rate, A. P. persuaded Carter Glass, chairman

of the Senate Committee on Banking, to include this clause in the act. A. P. was sure it would solve his problem and get back at Morgan. Jubilantly he wired one of his associates, Will Morrish: "Have succeeded in getting amendment in Glass Bill that will permit minority being represented on national bank boards." All in all, the Bank Act of 1933 contained important advantages for A. P. and justified his political support of the New Deal.

A. P.'s influence in Washington during the first years of the New Deal also extended to federal agencies such as the Reconstruction Finance Corporation. That was reflected in the crisis faced by California grape growers during the fall of 1933. Viticulturists were encountering difficult times not only because of the severity of the depression. The concurrent end of Prohibition also affected them negatively. As Americans once more were able to select the alcoholic beverage of their choice, the sales of wines plummeted. During Prohibition, wine consumption had increased substantially. But in 1933 prices dropped disastrously, at the wholesale level from $200 per ton of grapes to only $12. A. P. had a direct interest in the industry, since his bank had more than $6 million in loans outstanding to California vineyards. The growers needed help. A. P. himself went to Washington to persuade officials at the Reconstruction Finance Corporation to grant special credits to the California wine growers so that they might survive this difficult period of transition.

During the first Roosevelt administration A. P. worked hard to cultivate the major power brokers in the nation's capital and in California. In addition to making public statements in support of the president and visiting him in the White House, he was in frequent touch with Jim Farley, the president's political manager. He also had a close working relationship with Marriner Eccles (from Utah), one of the few western bankers in the Washington establishment. Eccles served as chairman of the Federal Reserve Board. A. P. had known Jesse Jones even before he became chairman of the Reconstruction Finance Corporation and had cordial relationships with him. James "Jeffy" O'Connor, the new comptroller of the currency, had been a close friend of A. P. ever since the former opened a legal practice in Los Angeles during the early 1920s. At that time he had become a law partner of William G. McAdoo, secretary of the treasury under President Wilson. When McAdoo was elected a U.S. senator from California in 1924, O'Connor became his protégé. At McAdoo's urging Roosevelt in 1933 appointed O'Connor as comptroller, providing A. P. with a sympathetic and influential supporter of branch banking in Washington.

Only minor disagreements marred A. P.'s love feast with the New Deal during the first two years of Roosevelt's presidency. In many ways, A. P. was a typical western banker: somewhat unorthodox, very flexible, and less inhibited by tradition than his eastern counterparts. That was certainly true of his policy on paying dividends. Throughout his career he favored payment of dividends to shareholders whenever possible, to retain the loyalty of the hundreds of thousands of small stockholders who had invested in his bank. Eastern bankers, however, and most federal regulators who were trained in eastern banking practices looked askance at such a policy, especially in times of depression. Thus A. P. raised many eyebrows when he announced that his bank would resume dividend payments on July 1, 1933. In the aftermath of the bank holiday proclaimed by President Roosevelt in March 1933, Comptroller O'Connor had recommended to all banks that they suspend dividends so as to build up their reserves. But A. P. had a small profit to report for his banks in 1933 and delighted in being contrary and somewhat of a showman. It was his firm belief that payment of dividends would boost the morale of his stockholders and would help to dispel the gloom that needed to be lifted if economic recovery was to be stimulated. Still, when national bank examiners went over the books of the Bank of America in January 1934, they questioned the wisdom of the policy, as well as his bookkeeping practices. Mostly they believed that he placed unrealistic values on real estate holdings. A. P. argued, however, that conditions in California were very different from those in Chicago or New York. Nevertheless, the examiners forced A. P. to alter his accounting standards so that they would conform more closely to federal guidelines.

Clearly, the technical aspects of A. P.'s banking practices were subject to various interpretations, but there is no doubt that these disputes also underlined the different psychologies of eastern and western bankers. Since the days of Andrew Jackson, easterners had tended to look somewhat askance at western banks, which they considered to be weak and irresponsible, and far more unstable than their eastern counterparts. To some extent such a perception had a basis in fact, but by the 1930s, when the West was more developed, it also reflected a cultural lag on the part of eastern financiers. In the 1930s the perception of the West as a colony of the East was still quite strong, and the eastern image of the West as an underdeveloped region quite common. It was not surprising, therefore, that bankers as well as government regulators, almost all of whom received their training and experience in eastern or eastern-oriented institutions, looked suspiciously at western banking practices, especially those of unorthodox bankers like A. P.

Also unlike many eastern bankers, A. P. decided to throw his support behind the New Deal's effort to reform the banking system, a prime objective of the Banking Act of 1935. Many major Wall Street financiers such as J. P. Morgan, Winthrop Aldrich, and James P. Warburg opposed the measure. They were especially concerned about increasing the powers of the Federal Reserve Board in Washington over the twelve regional Federal Reserve Banks, powers that threatened to diminish their own influence. In contrast, bankers who were not part of the Wall Street establishment, especially A. P. and Marriner Eccles, welcomed the diminution of the impact that New York financiers had on the nation's banks. As A. P. noted succinctly:

> It is true that one of the purposes of the Banking Bill is to lessen the authority of bankers to determine the monetary policies of the country, but it should be emphasized that bankers at large have had very little voice in the determination of such policies in the past. The group that has exerted the predominant influence has been the New York bankers. . . . Personally, I would rather that this power be exercised by a public body in the public interest than by the New York banking fraternity. . . . [The bill] is not a radical document sprung from the brains of theorists, but deep rooted in 20 years of practical experience with the Federal Reserve Act as tested by the worst depression in history.

The administration placed great value on A. P.'s support. "Greatly appreciate your statement," Eccles wired A. P. And he added, "It turned out better than I had reason to expect, and we gained not only all the essentials which we desired but . . . much more than I imagined would be conceded. . . . I doubt if we would have been successful against the great weight of banking opinion but for the fact that a few voices—all too few—and yours most notably, were raised in behalf of the bill." And in September 1935 Roosevelt himself wrote A. P. a grateful letter in which he noted:

> It is refreshing to know that some who occupy high places in the business and financial realms can remember the conditions as they existed several years ago and today can realize the changes for betterment that have come to us as a nation.
> I have read several newspaper reports of the statements you made

in this connection. Naturally, your observation that business in the Far West has shown such remarkable improvement and, in some sections, "is back where it was before the depression," pleases me much. . . . I expect to be in your State within a week or so and hope very much that it will be possible for us to meet once again.

When Roosevelt did visit southern California, A. P. remained in the north to strike a nonpartisan pose, advising Farley to provide for a nonpolitical reception committee. In late November, however, A. P. was in Washington, D.C., where the president invited him to dinner at the White House.

The Banking Act of 1935 was a comprehensive measure that did much to increase federal authority over the nation's banks. In the initial drafts of the bill, A. P.'s lobbyist had been able to insert a provision to encourage branch banking. That would have allowed the Bank of America to absorb Transamerica banks in Nevada and Oregon. But this section aroused the hostility of Secretary of the Treasury Henry Morgenthau, Jr., who insisted on its elimination. The three major sections that A. P. supported included the increase of the Federal Reserve Board's powers, an increase of federal deposit insurance to $5,000 for accounts in commercial banks, and authorization for new types of commercial paper that Federal Reserve Banks could utilize as collateral for loans.

With the moderate improvement of economic conditions during the first Roosevelt administration, A. P. devoted most of his energies to strengthening his bank's condition. The task was by no means easy. In the course of the decade, however, he succeeded in steering the institution so as to achieve recovery and some modest growth. Under his aegis the bank entered new spheres such as automobile sales, installment financing, and collaboration with federal housing programs. At the same time, the bank expanded its already major involvement with agribusiness and the movie industry in Hollywood. Gradually, as conditions warranted, A. P. also established new branches. Through such means A. P. was able to restore the bank to health, although his primary objective of establishing a nationwide branch banking system eluded him among the many tribulations of the Great Depression. Yet he revealed his still uncanny knack for taking advantage of contemporary social and economic trends.

Distinctively western was A. P.'s sensitivity to a vast consumer market and his policy of liberalizing his bank's loans for automobiles. In the 1930s almost 60 percent of car buyers bought their vehicles on the installment plan. During the depression most banks considered such loans very risky. Consequently most motorists turned to finance companies, who charged them between 15 and 30 percent interest annually. But as A. P. and Mario looked about for new sources of income, they decided to tap into this business. Between 1931 and 1935 they were not overly successful because, in addition to bad times, as Mario noted: "We handled it like bankers, whereas it requires people trained in finance company methods."

After 1935, however, automobile financing became an important source of bank profits. A. P. embarked on an extensive advertising campaign, taking out ads in newspapers, sponsoring innumerable radio spots, and plastering billboards throughout California. "Today 266 cars will be financed by the Bank of America," one blurb proclaimed. "Every five minutes another Bank of America financed car," declared another. Finance companies were clearly unhappy about this new competition. Their representatives lobbied hard with automobile dealers up and down the state, urging them to dissuade their customers from utilizing Bank of America loans because allegedly they were unsound. Yet the Bank of America's lower rates wooed tens of thousands of new customers to its branches. During the second half of the 1930s, the bank was second only to General Motors Acceptance Corporation in financing car purchases in California. These totaled $20 million annually for the bank, or 9 percent of the state's auto financing. By 1940 the Bank of America had become preeminent in the field, undercutting most of its competitors and providing exceptionally efficient service.

A. P.'s methods continued to shock many in the field of banking. His solicitation of loans and widespread advertising were not yet in the repertoire of most traditional bankers at the time. They viewed his policies with disdain and distrust. As the *American Banker,* a major trade journal, noted: "The Bank of America uses its advertising as a straight merchandising medium. It sells 'loans' just as American Tobacco Company sells Lucky Strikes. It never deviates and it never lets up. As a result, it is doubtful that there is a single literate person in California who has not heard of the willingness of the Bank of America to lend money."

In seeking to tap mass markets, A. P. also encouraged the extension of a very large volume of small loans. He instructed his branch managers to grant loans even when not much collateral was available, other than a person's good reputation, or his or her future prospects.

In this manner A. P. and the Bank of America entered into the lives of millions of Californians. One young man, for example, secured a loan to buy a twenty-two-foot python snake, which he hoped would appear in a motion picture. Countless others borrowed to finance the birth of a new child. In many instances A. P. would donate five dollars to the parents in a newly established savings account for the potential young depositor of the future. The bank also encouraged the thousands of sardine fishermen in California to take out loans to tide them over the difficult months between fishing seasons. Most of the small loans ranged from $100 to $1,000. The seventeen thousand finance companies in California who had carried such business were visibly concerned about the intrusion of the Bank of America into a domain that they had long considered to be their own. But A. P. established his small-loan department in 1929 and was determined to capture much of the market. Despite the depression, by 1933 he had completed 30,000 such loans. Then his concentrated advertising campaigns had a striking effect as by 1938 the bank was handling 600,000 such loans annually, totaling more than $616 million. Through charging lower rates than his competitors and by providing friendly and efficient service, A. P. secured the edge.

Under A. P.'s guidance, the bank also embarked on a deliberate policy of stimulating new enterprises, largely in the realm of small business. He designed his program especially for those who did not usually qualify for open lines of credit or who hoped to expand existing operations. In previous years such enterprises were denied credit by banks and had been forced to turn to finance companies to secure needed capital, usually at exorbitant rates. A. P. decided, however, that he would solicit this type of loan, which most other banks avoided, with a special passion and aggressiveness. From 1937 to 1940, in particular, he did much to stimulate industries such as jewelry, oil well supplies, furniture, and lumber. He also played a significant role in encouraging the fledgling textile and clothing in-dustry in southern California, which quickly grew to major propor-tions. Encouraged by the glamor provided by Hollywood, Los Angeles in these years became an important national center for the manufacture of leisure and sports clothing. As output increased ten-fold in the late 1930s, the Bank of America became the major financier of the industry. Within a short time the bank built up a corps of experts who worked closely with people in the industry, advising on markets, styles, and color. A. P.'s policy of encouraging small business earned him the plaudits of Jesse Jones of the Reconstruction Finance Corporation. "It is refreshing to see a bank willing to go to the trouble or originating loans to its own community," Jones noted in July 1938, "rather than confining itself largely to buying 'tailor made' credits in the way of low-yielding bonds and so-called commercial paper by others."

To generate new business A. P. also actively expanded the bank's loans to small home buyers. His efforts were greatly stimulated by the Federal Housing Act of 1934, which provided for federal guarantees for new and renovated homes. Under the FHA program A. P.'s bank made more loans than any other institution in the United States, totaling more than one million such loans between 1934 and 1950.

The bank continued its close relations with California farmers. In 1936 it created a commodity loan department, which advanced $40 million to farm cooperatives during the next four years. In addition, the bank extended about $33 million in emergency lines of credit to individual farmers. Much to A. P.'s dismay, his bank also acquired about four thousand farms through foreclosure. He tried to sell these through a new subsidiary, California Lands, although he encountered problems in finding buyers. In some cases the bank leased properties to individuals who sometimes qualified for loans allowing for future purchase. Most small farmers, however, found these to be trying times.

This was even truer of California's migratory farm workers, whose numbers increased greatly in the 1930s and who viewed A. P. and his bank as natural enemies. In view of A. P.'s close connections with all segments of California agribusiness, he was vulnerable to charges of exploitation. Some of the accusations were made by the *People's World,* California's Communist newspaper. Not always scrupulous in its checking of facts, the organ accused the Bank of America of conducting an unholy war against farm labor. More serious were the veiled references to the bank made by John Steinbeck in his enormously popular *Grapes of Wrath* (1939), in which he charged a fictional Bank of the West (closely resembling the Bank of America) with contributing mightily to the dilemmas of the Joad family, the fictional victims in the novel.

Less subtle was Carey McWilliams, a gifted popular writer, who in his *Factories in the Field* (1940), an indictment of California agribusiness and its treatment of farm workers, declared that the Bank of America controlled 50 percent of all farm lands in northern California and in the Central Valley. As McWilliams wrote in his impassioned volume: "When one realizes that approximately 50 per cent of the farm lands in Central and Northern California are controlled by one institution—the Bank of America—the irony of these 'embattled' farmers defending their 'homes' against shysters becomes apparent" (p. 233). A. P. and his staff rushed to defend the bank against these accusations and presented evidence to prove that the actual figure was 3.6 percent. Although McWilliams made a retraction in a private letter to the bank, he did not make an explicit statement on the correction in later printings of the book. A. P. was greatly concerned about possible damage to his public image and that of the bank. But the storm blew over quickly, without visible effects.

A considerable share of the bank's profits came from its close involvement with the movie industry. Like other forms of business, motion pictures suffered under the impact of the depression. Paramount Pictures, the largest of Hollywood's studios, declared bankruptcy in 1933. By then, Metro-Goldwyn-Mayer, RKO, United Artists, and Universal Pictures had already reorganized to avoid the same fate. As fewer people went to the movies in the first five years of the depression, the studios found that their revenues plummeted. In 1933 these totaled only one-half of what they had been before the crash.

But A. P. had had close ties to the movie makers for more than a decade and continued his cautious, but consistent, support. In 1933 he lent $3 million to Darryl Zanuck and Joseph Schenck (a director of the Bank of America) to organize a new company, known by 1935 as 20th Century Fox. His gamble was eminently successful, as the newcomer produced a string of major hits. Indeed, A. P. seemed to have a special sensitivity that enabled him to judge the potential of most films that he financed. He also granted large loans to Zanuck to produce six very profitable features, including *Bulldog Drummond Strikes Back* and *Cellini*.

A. P. was closely involved with many of the famous Hollywood personalities of the period. He had a fine working relationship with Samuel B. Goldwyn and became a major backer for his *Arrowsmith*, *Stella Dallas*, and *Winning of Barbara Worth*. In 1932, during the depths of the depression, A. P. lent Goldwyn $1 million to produce *The Kid from Spain*, which starred Eddy Cantor. Despite the hard times, the film was a big success and made money for the producers. A. P. also profited from a succession of winners, for which he lent Goldwyn large sums, including the *Goldwyn Follies of 1938* and *Wuther-*

ing Heights. The legendary Cecil B. DeMille, another favorite A. P. client, received A. P.'s help in producing *Union Pacific* and *Cleopatra*, which were huge box office successes. In addition, Bank of America loans financed such hits as *It Happened One Night* and *Mr. Smith Goes to Washington* at Columbia Pictures, *King Kong* at RKO, and *Mutiny on the Bounty* at Metro-Goldwyn-Mayer. During the 1930s A. P.'s bank financed more than one hundred films, extending more than $55 million in credits to the industry.

Even during the difficult years of the depression, A. P. at times took chances with untried ventures, such as those of Walt Disney. At the time Disney was an unknown cartoon animator and producer of short features and was known as a rather unorthodox filmmaker. A. P. had his first contacts with him in 1923, when he granted him small loans. A. P. liked *Mickey Mouse* and provided funds for other shorts such as *Steamboat Willie, Silly Symphonies,* and *Three Little Pigs* in 1930.

As Disney developed his artistic concepts, he increasingly considered the making of a longer film. While on a trip to Paris in 1935, he crystallized his ideas. Disney noted that theater owners there often showed half a dozen feature cartoons in succession, usually to packed houses. "The short subject had always gotten the short end of the stick in Hollywood," he said in later years. "You were always the one they could do away with." When he returned to Hollywood, he decided to embark on the production of a Grimm brothers fairy tale, *Little Snow White.* Disney was a perfectionist, however, and by the end of 1936 had already spent $500,000 on the venture, when he ran out of funds. In this dilemma he turned to Attilio Giannini, who was in charge of Bank of America loans in Hollywood. Attilio was extremely negative. Movie patrons were unlikely to pay to see a full-length animated cartoon, he told Disney, particularly one starring a collection of dwarfs. The dejected Disney was desperate, however. He decided to go to San Francisco to plead with A. P., whom he did not know personally. A. P. usually left much of the movie business to Attilio without his own personal involvement. Since he so warmly disliked his brother, however, he never let a chance slip by to humiliate him or to upstage him. Moreover, he was impressed by Disney and promptly offered him the needed money. Before Disney completed the film late in 1937, the Bank of America had lent him $1.7 million, a staggering sum at the time.

The rest is history. A. P.'s enormous gamble paid off handsomely, for the picture was a huge success. Just in its first showing it grossed $22 million. Thereafter, A. P. provided Disney with ample funds, with which he produced some of his greatest classics, including *Dumbo, Fantasia,* and *Pinocchio.*

The Disney films were not the only blockbusters in which A. P. had a hand. He profited greatly from a venture begun by David O. Selznick, Louis B. Mayer's son-in-law. In 1935 Selznick formed his own production company, and in the following year paid $50,000 for an as yet unpublished novel by an unknown author. The novel was *Gone with the Wind,* and the author was Margaret Mitchell. Production costs of what grew to be a major spectacle far exceeded expectations, however. Unable to secure financing from private investors, Selznick appealed to A. P. for funds, inviting him to the set in Culver City. A. P. came, was impressed, and forthwith lent him $1.6 million. It was a sage investment indeed.

As depression conditions improved slightly in the course of the decade, A. P. was able to continue at least a modest expansion of his branches. By 1940 the bank had also made significant gains in increasing deposits. In 1938 it had almost two million accounts, one for every 3.5 persons in California. As deposits doubled between 1930 and 1940, the institution was able to increase its earnings substantially. That did not assuage A. P.'s restlessness, however. He was still in pursuit of his main goal of establishing nationwide banking. Although this goal eluded him during the depression, he was able to add seventy-five new branches to his system, forty-five through purchases and thirty that were brand new. Thus, while the economic crisis interfered with A. P.'s grandiose plans for national and global banking, he was eminently successful in guiding his institution through the difficult problems of the depression and nursing it back to health.

Nevertheless, A. P.'s banking practices continued to arouse concern among competitors as well as government regulators. The comptroller of the currency, who supervised national banks, and also the Federal Deposit Insurance Corporation questioned many of the new types of loans A. P. inaugurated during the 1930s. Whereas A. P. often listed the character of his clients as an asset, the national bank examiners were loath to recognize such an intangible. They were also concerned with his loans to Hollywood. Bank examiners trained in eastern banking practices were not too familiar with the motion picture industry and often questioned the value of film negatives, which A. P. accepted as collateral for loans to film producers. The lag between A. P.'s introduction of new banking practices and their acceptance by other financiers, as well as differences between eastern and western perceptions of sound banking, continued to create friction. Just as he had experienced problems with state regulators in the 1920s, so hostility between him and New Deal regulators developed in the 1930s.

Much of this hostility crystallized around Secretary of the Treasury Henry Morganthau, who was opposed to large-scale expansion of branch banking and who was apprehensive about A. P.'s banking methods. To some extent the antagonisms were also personal. As Jesse Jones remarked: "There was no love lost between Mr. Giannini and Secretary Morgenthau." But broader policy issues were also at stake. In 1937 President Roosevelt embarked on an antitrust campaign. Not only did the Department of Justice under Assistant Secretary Thurman Arnold inaugurate a series of antitrust suits, but the president also appointed the Temporary National Economic Committee to investigate economic concentration. A. P.'s policy of expanding the number of his branches and of concentrating bank resources thus flew directly in the face of the New Deal's antimonopoly program. As an important member of the administration, Morgenthau was obligated to carry out its mission. In addition to his concern about A. P.'s increasing dominance in western banking, Morgenthau was alarmed by A. P.'s sometimes freewheeling and unorthodox banking practices. These included the payment of dividends during depression years, acceptance of various types of collateral for security against loans that were questionable in the eyes of eastern bankers, and debatable bookkeeping practices, especially in regard to the valuation of real estate.

A. P. accentuated these differences when early in 1937 he lobbied hard for new legislation that would make it possible for him to establish regional banking in the West, a law that would allow him to transcend state borders. His holding company, Transamerica, already owned banks in Washington, Oregon, Nevada, and Arizona. If the Bank of America could take over the direct operation of these banks, he could integrate them more closely into his system. Unfortunately, A. P.'s timing was not propitious, since the administration was just then inaugurating its campaign against economic concentration. Early in 1937 A. P. prevailed upon Senator William G. McAdoo to sponsor two bills that would accomplish his objectives. One was designed to allow National Banks to operate branches everywhere in the Federal Reserve District in which they had their main offices. The other prohibited holding companies from owning more than 10 percent of the stock of any bank that belonged to the Federal Reserve system. A. P. favored the abolition of bank holding companies so that banks would be allowed to operate directly in more than one state. But with the new wave of strong antimonopoly sentiment and Morgenthau's strong opposition, neither measure received much support.

Morgenthau also rejected A. P.'s applications for new branches. At that point A. P. tried his familiar policy of bypass. He appealed to Marvin McIntire, the president's secretary, to order the comptroller to issue the necessary permits. The president remained mute on the request, however, and A. P.'s maneuver hardly endeared him to Morgenthau. At the same time, the comptroller's bank examiners were investigating the bank's books, where they found much to criticize.

By 1937 Morgenthau sought to exercise more stringent controls over A. P.'s banking practices. Since the comptroller-general enjoyed considerable independence, the treasury secretary intended to impose his more direct control over the office. That move was opposed as well by Marriner Eccles of the Federal Reserve Board, friendly also to branch banking. But Morgenthau was successful in forcing the resignation of the incumbent comptroller, J. F. T. O'Connor. Instead, he selected as a personal choice Marshall R. Diggs as acting comptroller in 1937. The latter instructed his National Bank examiners to continue their conservative approach to investigating lending policies and bookkeeping practices of banks under their jurisdiction.

Next, Morgenthau hoped to chastise various bank managements, including those at the Bank of America, through adverse reports on their condition. In September 1938 the examiners swooped down on A. P.'s system. On September 13, 1938, just a few hours before a regularly scheduled meeting of the bank's board of directors in Los Angeles, R. E. A. Palmer, the resident national bank examiner there, called Mario Giannini to tell him that he would attend the session. As A. P. was presiding over the otherwise uneventful meeting, Palmer strode in to read a message from Comptroller Diggs that proved to be a bombshell. Diggs declared:

> In view of the unsatisfactory asset condition of the bank, of real estate in excess of forty million dollars carried in loans and discounts and . . .

of other items carried in assets of questionable value . . . it is imperative
that the earnings of the bank be used to write off and reduce book
value of such assets. Notwithstanding the condition as outlined above
and the fact that the dividend policy has been repeatedly criticized, the
dividend rate had been repeatedly increased. . . . In the opinion of the
comptroller of the currency the declaration of any dividends at this
time would . . . [be] an unsafe and unsound practice. . . . Accordingly
the comptroller . . . warns the bank to discontinue such unsafe and
unsound practice.

A. P. was embarrassed and also dumbfounded. Forthwith he requested a hearing before the Federal Reserve Board. Meanwhile,
Morgenthau also rebuked him publicly and charged that by declaring
a dividend he was defying the comptroller. The secretary also questioned the declared asset value of the bank and expressed his belief
that it was undercapitalized. A. P. eagerly hoped to make a detailed
reply to these allegations. In part, the dispute reflected differences
between eastern and western perceptions of what constituted sound
banking, particularly in relation to valuation of real estate. On that
matter the bank's statement noted:

> Real estate is the backbone of the country. It represents a greater
> proportion of the wealth of the country than does any other form of
> property. From it as a source of taxation the state, county, and munici-
> pal governments obtain their chief revenues. Ownership of real estate
> gives stability to the citizen. . . . It is necessary for us to satisfy the
> diverse credit requirements of all the communities which we serve. . . .
> We therefore feel that the examiners should consider our real estate
> security in the light of the principles which should govern a sound
> savings bank practice.

A. P.'s fury knew no bounds and brought out some of his less
desirable characteristics, such as a streak of anti-Semitism. He had
maintained close relationships with Jews for many years, including
such movie moguls as Harry Cohn, Louis B. Mayer, and Joseph
Schenck, the last two of whom served on his board of directors for
many years. But just as he had at various times expressed admiration
for Benito Mussolini (for whom he also provided profitable financial
transactions), so his feud with Morgenthau and Jewish bankers like
Eugene Meyer and Herbert Fleischhacker brought out his baser
instincts. Nor did the increasing anti-Semitism of the Italian dictator
seem to bother A. P. In October 1938 A. P. made an emotional scene
at a meeting of his board of directors in Los Angeles. He screamed
and shouted about the Jew sonofabitch Morgenthau, promising that

this was one goddamn Jew who was in for a fight to the finish. His waterfront language was not unfamiliar to members of the board. But this time the Jewish directors Mayer and Schenck got up in disgust and left the room. And within a few days they resigned their positions on the board. As Schenck wrote on October 11, 1938, in a measured letter to A. P.:

> There are two reasons why I am resigning. The number one reason is because of the expression that you made regarding the Jews being against you. I know you are possibly of a suspicious mind and in looking for a reason for the unjustified criticisms which have been made by the comptroller's office you discovered the international fall guy—the Jew. However, I happen to be a Jew and it didn't sit well with me. It was very embarrassing and I, therefore, feel that I am better off out of the bank.

If A. P. was personally sorry about the incident, he did not show it, for he did not apologize. But he was concerned about his public image.

News of his bigoted remarks leaked out quickly. Within a few months they were discussed in various publications such as a *Fortune* article in June 1939. When critical letters poured into the bank, A. P. sought to mend fences. "The article to which you refer," he wrote to one of his irate depositors, "was as much a surprise to me as it was to my friends of all races and creeds. . . . The names of certain government officials . . . were used, because I have every reason to believe these persons are responsible for the persecution now going on against my son and myself. It just happens that several of the men mentioned were Jewish, but my remarks were made without the slightest thought of any religion or any race but were predicated on the fact that they were the individuals active in this and former unjust attacks."

Always concerned about the image of his bank, A. P. also issued a press release that received wide coverage in California newspapers on December 10 and 12, 1938. Designed as a Christmas message, he warned his employees against the "vice of intolerance." The United States was a melting pot, he noted, and had produced "and alloy from which has been forged the stuff that is America. . . . It is important . . . that we practice tolerance in this country as never before, and that we steadfastly fight against any form of racial or religious prejudice or hatred."

The whole affair obviously worsened his relationship with Morgenthau. Convinced that the secretary was spreading rumors that his bank was unsound and that Morgenthau was out to ruin him, A. P. sent him a rather heated telegram in which he ranted: "Don't you think, Mr. Secretary, that your continued unwarranted and unjustifiable smearing has gone on far enough?" That led to an angry response from Morgenthau, who felt that he was "impelled to write in the hope that the tactics of personal vituperation you adopted in this telegram do not represent your considered judgment but were prompted by momentary anger. . . . There are matters of grave import pending between the Comptroller of the Currency . . . and the financial institutions of which you are the responsible head. Let us not muddy the waters by personal animus."

After this heated exchange both sides adopted a more conciliatory mood. Through conferences and letters A. P. gradually tried to smooth the waters. As soon as President Roosevelt selected a new comptroller, Preston Delano (a distant relative of the chief executive), A. P. approached him with offers to work out a mutually satisfactory agreement. He sent his son Mario, together with two other associates, to Washington to work out a compromise. A. P. agreed to increase the bank's capital stock and to pay dividends only in relation to the maintenance of a 1 to 10 ratio of capital funds to deposits. Jesse Jones, the chairman of the Reconstruction Finance Corporation, who had brought the two sides together, reportedly told Mario on the phone: "You've a great bank. Go home and tend to business, and forget the situation here."

But Morgenthau was not wholly satisfied with these terms and extended his attack. After sending reports of his National Bank examiners to the Securities and Exchange Commission, he encouraged that agency to file fraud charges against the Transamerica Corporation for its stock issuance practices during 1937. Over the next few years A. P. was able to ward off this accusation in the courts. He hired a well-known New Dealer, Donald Richberg (who had once directed the National Recovery Administration) to press his case. It took almost a decade, but in 1947 the federal courts dismissed the charges. Meanwhile, in November 1939 National Bank examiners continued to accuse the Bank of America of unsound banking practices. Although both A. P. and Mario journeyed to Washington to refute Comptroller Delano's accusations in person, they were unsuccessful.

Yet A. P. showed the same resourcefulness that had made him one of the nation's leading bankers. He now decided to remove the Bank

America from the Treasury Department's jurisdiction. That he could do by transforming his banks into state-chartered institutions. He also asked the Federal Reserve Board, where his friend Marriner Eccles still held sway, to make an independent investigation of his bank. But A. P. never quite understood that between 1935 and 1940 Eccles and other western bankers, as well as ardent New Dealers, had a very real fear of monopolistic tendencies that the Bank of America personified in the field of banking. In his request A. P. denounced Morgenthau's actions and the Securities and Exchange Commission's investigation. "Publication of unproven charges against our bank," he declared, "would have destroyed a bank whose good will was less strongly entrenched." And he advised Mario to take a tough stance against Morgenthau. "Strike from the shoulder," he said—"nothing in the way of apologies, patronizing, or humbling ourselves." Mario did just that. Speaking to a meeting of stockholders on January 9, 1940, he told them:

> Were it not for the privilege that surrounds his office, Mr. Morgenthau would not dare to act as he has. We do not propose to relinquish our self-respect and submit to his high-handed tactics. . . . We shall continue to contend for honest treatment and fair consideration of your Bank's affairs, and civil treatment of its directors and officers. If this cannot be accomplished rationally, and if it later appears that Mr. Morgenthau is to be permitted to continue to use his position arbitrarily to harass your bank, we may suggest that you consider its conversion to a state bank. It is not necessary to be a national bank in order to be a member of the Federal Deposit Insurance Corporation or the Federal Reserve System.

And in a telegram to Comptroller Delano, Mario declared his formal intention as he wrote: "We propose promptly to initiate [reconversion] proceedings. Please advise us whether or not there are any formalities prescribed by . . . your office relating to such proceedings." Such a threat intimidated Morgenthau and other treasury officials, in view of the size of A. P.'s system. When Mario returned to Washington in February 1940, he was able to work out an acceptable agreement over outstanding issues with Treasury Department staff. The terms were published on March 15, 1940. Meanwhile, changing conditions were working in favor of the Gianninis, especially the outbreak of the Second World War. By this time the Roosevelt administration had quietly shelved its antimonopoly campaign. Instead, it shifted its main energies to the defense mobilization program.

Within this broader context, Morgenthau found his feud with A. P. untimely and unproductive.

By the end of the decade A. P. could be satisfied that under his general guidance Mario had steered the Bank of America through the difficult times of depression. He had encountered serious obstacles toward the achievement of his dream of establishing nationwide banking, of course. Most significant was the economic crisis, which did not provide a suitable context for his endeavors. In addition, fears of monopoly and economic concentration aroused a sufficient number of opponents, who became increasingly fearful of his goals. His unorthodox and often peremptory banking methods aroused concern within and without the financial community. To some extent regional differences, between eastern and western conceptions of banking, created frictions and impediments that tended to stifle some of his ambitions. Nevertheless, in 1940 the bank was much larger and stronger than it had been a decade before. As in earlier stages of A. P.'s career, luck continued to smile on his endeavors. Just as he felt stymied by the opposition of New Deal regulators, the economic context in which he had been operating changed significantly. When the nation geared up for war and Americans shed many of the views they had held in the depression era, he found that once again times were propitious for the expansion of his treasured institution.

CHAPTER 6

In Active Retirement, 1940–1949

ALTHOUGH A. P. withdrew somewhat from day-to-day operations of his bank between 1940 and his death in 1949, he continued
to be a major presence in guiding its major policies. During the
World War II years he took full advantage of the economic boom
spawned by mobilization. The return of prosperity did a great deal
to allow him to expand his bank operations further. In keeping with
earlier policies that had proved successful, he continued to focus on
the financing of small business, even as the bank became more involved in financing large corporations than it had in earlier years. He
also was able to extend the number of his branches. In contrast to
the First World War, when his bank had only played a very minor
role in providing funds for conversion to wartime production on the
Pacific Coast, between 1940 and 1945 his institution was a major force
in facilitating the enormous expansion of the shipbuilding and aircraft
industries. For the first time in his life he could rival or equal the
major Wall Street banks in underwriting the extraordinary growth
of industry in California. In 1945 he certainly had not achieved all of
his dreams for the bank. But he could take satisfaction in having
realized one of his main goals—the emergence of the Bank of America
as the West's largest financial institution.

As he peered into the future in 1940, A. P. planned a slightly slower
pace for himself, for he was now entering his seventies. "I want to
withdraw a little further," he reflected, "and leave more of the active
leadership in younger hands." He still expected to direct the bank,
however, like "the family watchdog, ready to growl at any sign of
danger from without, and ready to bark at you if I find any turning
away from the ideals on which this institution was built. . . . We, as
a bank, could never have survived the assaults of the past two years
or more if we had not been clean and sound, with no guilty secrets.
I have never locked my desk or a single drawer in it. I have nothing
to hide, nor has the bank." By the end of 1945 the Bank of America

was in a preeminent position to participate in the Pacific Coast's postwar boom. But by then the bank had achieved global eminence and was operating on a worldwide scale.

During the Second World War A. P. found that he could pursue the interest of his bank at the same time that he could contribute to the mobilization effort. The enormous influx of people into California made it possible for him to extend his branches and to expand the size of the bank further. The very rapid growth of business and industry afforded him unusual opportunities for imaginative innovations. Some of this was in spheres such as small-business financing, in which the bank was already well established. Other programs stimulated large-scale manufacturing. In many ways the war provided A. P. with an exciting arena of which he took full advantage.

Among these opportunities A. P. discerned was subcontracting, a practice that did much to stimulate manufacturing on the Pacific Coast. Many of the production increases in shipbuilding and aircraft were accomplished through the assembly of prefabricated parts. These were usually made by thousands of small-business enterprises—subcontractors who delivered their parts to large assembly centers, usually shipyards and airframe factories. But as small businesses converted to war production and secured government contracts, they needed local financing. This is where the Bank of America came in. With its far-flung branches it was in an excellent position to take advantage of the situation. A. P. was ecstatic about it because it meshed so well with his own business plans and with his predilection for helping the little fellow. Moreover, he believed that extensive decentralization would avoid many of the problems faced by congested boomtowns. As he noted in October 1941: "It means the continued functioning of local industry, maintenance of payrolls, stabilization of employment for the skilled in established surroundings of which he and his family are an important part, greater production for defense, and a big step toward cushioning the readjustments which must follow the ultimate curtailment of the defense program."

Largely because of A. P.'s urgings, in November 1941 Governor Culbert Olson called a conference in Sacramento to coordinate statewide activities to promote subcontracting on the local level. In his characteristic enterprising fashion A. P. arranged for dozens of local meetings on the same theme organized by his branches to coincide with the conference in the state capital. By the time of Pearl Harbor the Bank of America was deeply involved in a massive campaign revolving around the slogan "Convert your plant to national defense." In addition, the bank's officers traveled about the state to organize small pools of manufacturers. Such pools could qualify for federally guaranteed loans, which federal agencies offered to prime contractors (but not to individual small subcontractors). A. P. took special pride in the fact that one of the first of these to be established was in his home town of San Jose. There Verne C. Richards, an officer of the local Bank of America branch, became its chief adviser. Good patriotism was also good business. The bank loaned the association $70,000 as a start and promised an additional $500,000.

A. P. was especially happy to nurture firms he had supported for many years and had sustained during the hard days of the depression. One such example was the Solar Aircraft Company of San Diego. In 1944 it was manufacturing stainless steel exhaust manifolds for B-29 bombers. During the 1930s the company had been barely able to survive by making bookends and frying pans. In those critical years the Bank of America had kept it afloat with small but strategic loans. In 1939 A. P. made it possible for the firm to convert to defense production with $100,000 in credits. Within the next five years the company secured federal contracts in excess of $90 million. The Bank of America continued to aid in the expansion, lending $4.2 million during the war years. When in 1945 the enterprise shifted to manufacturing components for jet aircraft, a syndicate of New York as well as western banks provided them with more than $12.5 million in loans. The Bank of America contributed $8 million. It was the kind of success story that reflected A. P.'s gratification with his work as a banker.

A. P. was also heavily involved with large prime contractors in major California industries such as aircraft. The costs in building new plants for this industry exceeded $150 million. Private capital supplied $79 million, while the federal government provided the rest. The big manufacturers in the state—Douglas, Lockheed, North American, Ryan, Consolidated Vultee—undertook extensive subcontracting throughout the seventeen western states. Concentrating on the making of airframes, they assembled thousands of parts, and Detroit automakers sent the engines. Much of the financing for this expansion was underwritten by eastern banks, who commanded vast amounts of capital that were needed within brief periods. This growth of aircraft manufactures in California gave A. P. an opportunity to get his foot in the door in the arena of syndicate financing. For the first time in his career, he was able to join with Wall Street syndicates in developing western industry. A. P. designated Vice-Chairman Francis S. Baer as his representative in syndicate ventures. The breakthrough for him came with the first such project—the Consolidated Vultee Corporation of San Diego—which was also one of A. P.'s largest depositors. Until 1941 the company was totally dependent on Wall Street for loans or investment capital. Its major financier was the Chase National Bank of New York, which organized a $200 million pool. In 1942 eastern financiers for the first time allowed the Bank of America to participate. A. P. was enormously gratified to know that the $15 million his bank contributed was equal to the sum lent by Chase. Once the ice had been broken, A. P. found that his bank achieved new stature in the banking world. Within a year eastern banks invited him to participate in syndicated loans to corporations like General Motors, Chrysler, Lockheed, Westinghouse, and RCA. The war gave the Bank of America an exposure it had not enjoyed in the previous decade.

To facilitate more war contracts for small-business enterprises, A. P. in November 1941 established the Bank of America Defense Information office in Washington, D.C. Located in the Mayflower Hotel, its staff regularly made the rounds of procurement agencies in the nation's capital to solicit work for California's subcontractors, and in particular for clients of the Bank of America. During the first six months of operation, the office garnered about two thousand such contracts, totaling $42 million. The experience convinced A. P. that a government corporation to perform such functions on the national level would be highly desirable. In March of 1942 he sent a representative to testify before the U.S. Senate Special Committee on Small Business to urge the creation of such an agency. By June 1942 the War Production Board established a division to direct federal contracts to small business. It came to play a visible role in wartime and gradually evolved into the Smaller War Plants Corporation.

As a means of accelerating mobilization, A. P. urged federal guarantees for bank loans to small contractors seeking to convert to war production. It was good business and at the same time served the national defense effort. A. P. first broached the idea to his old friend at the Federal Reserve Board, Marriner Eccles. He found him sympathetic. In its own effort to boost production, the Federal Reserve Board in May 1942 issued its Regulation V. This provided for full government guarantees for loans made by banks to small contractors.

Under this program Bank of America loans covered almost every aspect of the mobilization program. It was obviously of great advantage to banks—who took little risk—while at the same time it stimulated manufactures.

Typical of the loans made by the Bank of America under Regulation V was one under which it lent $136,000 to the Technical Oil Tool Company to manufacture tachometers for Norden bombsights in southern California. The bank lent $500,000 to the Gillespie Furniture Company to make fuel drop tanks for airplanes. Under Bank of America guidance the Grayson Heat Control Company, a manufacturer of thermostats, converted to the fabrication of hydraulic controls for airplane wing flaps. The bank lent $500,000 to the Western Stove Company so that it could manufacture incendiary bombs. Cole of California—already well known for its bathing suits—received $325,000 to convert to the manufacture of parachutes. And A. P. personally directed a $1 million loan to Walt Disney for developing educational and propaganda films.

A. P. also brought his bank into working with prime contractors in the shipbuilding industry. Much of the financing for the construction of new shipyards came from the federal government—more than $400 million on the Pacific Coast. But the subcontractors hired by the large yards still required extensive loans, mainly from private banks. This was a sphere in which the Bank of America reaped a bonanza. Major shipbuilders included Calship, in the Los Angeles area, and the Kaiser installations in the San Francisco Bay area. Smaller operations aided by the Bank of America were yards in the interior of California. At Antioch and Stockton shipbuilders constructed wooden minesweepers, and those in Napa built oil barges. Thousands of contractors now became involved in making parts for prefabricated ships, manufacturing machinery, masts, boat houses, booms, and hoists. One major facility, the Mare Island Naval shipyard in Vallejo, itself employed more than 1,900 prime contractors and 300 subcontractors, spread out through California, Utah, Colorado, and Wyoming, involving more than 25,000 workers.

A. P. had known Henry J. Kaiser, the West's leading shipbuilder, since the 1920s. At that time Kaiser was mainly involved with road construction projects, for which he had approached A. P. for loans. From the very beginning the two men took a liking to each other. Both were dreamers of large dreams. Both were innovative and enthusiastic. Both relished great challenges. Both were builders, entrepreneurs whose imaginations knew few boundaries. Both were the sons of immigrants (Kaiser of German antecedents) who sprang from modest homes but who rose rapidly to great success. Once he had made contact with A. P., Kaiser quickly became a valued client. The Bank of America financed his road-building activities in such far-flung places as British Columbia and Cuba, financed his building of levees on the Mississippi River and laying of pipelines in California. A. P. was also behind Kaiser in his most important project before World War II, participating as one of the six companies in the construction of Boulder (Hoover) Dam. At the time this was the largest such structure in the world and attracted global attention. When Franklin Roosevelt went to the White House in March of 1933, Kaiser appeared there a month later to solicit federal funds for public works. Roosevelt did not know Kaiser but had been in touch with A. P., who gave Kaiser a letter of introduction to the president in which he noted:

> I wish to introduce to you Mr. Henry J. Kaiser of Bridge Builders, Inc., one of the low bidders on the San Francisco–Oakland Bay Bridge. He is also chairman of the Executive Committee of the Six Companies, who hold the contract on Boulder Dam.
>
> Mr. Kaiser is in Washington on matters pertaining to the Bay Bridge, and while there would like to consult with you. He is a man of outstanding ability, very highly thought of in this community, and has been a friend and customer of the bank since the first day he came to California.
>
> Any courtesies extended to him I shall greatly appreciate. Respectfully, A. P. Giannini.

A. P.'s support undoubtedly smoothed Kaiser's path. During the New Deal years he secured important federal contracts for building sections of Grand Coulee and Bonneville dams in the Pacific Northwest and Parker Dam in Arizona. He supplied all of the cement needed for completing Shasta Dam, another major project. The Bank of America lent Kaiser $7.5 million to finance part of the cost of Kaiser's new Permanente Cement Company in California, at the time (1939–41) the largest such facility in the world. Soon after it was completed, it came to be crucial not only in supplying cement necessary for the rebuilding of the damaged airfields at Pearl Harbor in 1942 but also in providing much of the cement used in the construction of air and naval bases on Pacific islands during World War II.

Kaiser was eager to aid the war effort in other ways as well. In 1941 he decided to embark on the fabrication of merchant ships, although he had never built a vessel in his life. Admiral Emery S. Land, chairman of the U.S. Maritime Commission, who was in charge of issuing contracts for merchant vessels, liked Kaiser's spirit, however, and in 1941 gave him a $40 million order for twenty-four ships. Based on the model of a British tramp steamer, these ten-thousand-ton carriers quickly became known as Liberty ships. Kaiser approached the challenge much as he had other large construction projects. He decided that organization, prefabrication, and mass-production assembly-line techniques would do the job. Although the U.S. Maritime Commission became Kaiser's major financier, the Bank of America served as his largest private lender. The bank also gave him credit so he could build new steel plants at Fontana, California, and a magnesium processing facility at Milpitas, in the San Francisco Bay area. Kaiser's credit line at the Bank of America exceeded $43 million.

A. P.'s bank was also a major purveyor of capital to other large West Coast shipbuilders. These included the Rheem Manufacturing Company of Richmond (which had other plants also in Houston, Chicago, New Orleans, and Newark, N.J.) and the old and well-known Moore Dry Dock Company, in Oakland (Alameda). W. A. Bechtel, an associate of Kaiser, established Marinship in Sausalito, California, one of the most efficient shipyards in the nation. He too became a valued customer of the Bank of America. These ventures inaugurated a new phase in Pacific Coast and western banking. For the first time, shipbuilding activities on the coast were financed by syndicates largely composed of western banks. This was a precedent-setting step that A. P. truly relished. Here western institutions were providing sufficient new investment capital to develop industrial growth in the region. Although the excitement of wartime frenzy overshadowed such a significant trend, it heralded a new phase in western economic growth by lessening western economic dependence on the concentrated power of the East. In that process A. P. played an important role. And in the autumn of his life he took tremendous satisfaction in the recognition that he had accomplished one aspect of his dream—national recognition for his bank—and for the economic prowess of the region from which it sprang.

The development of the new wartime industries precipitated another major population boom in the West. Cities like San Diego doubled in population, Los Angeles gained more than 800,000 newcomers; the San Francisco Bay area became a conglomeration of chaotic boomtowns, of which Richmond—which expanded from 20,000 people in 1940 to 160,000 in 1943—was the most striking. This influx of individuals from all over the United States created a housing shortage such as California had rarely experienced in previous years. People slept in trailers or garages, often ten to a room, took turns in "hot beds," or simply camped out in the open. Although the federal government built 100,000 new housing units in public housing projects, demand always outran supply. This shortage created additional opportunities for the Bank of America to expand its operations. Between 1940 and 1945 it made almost one million residential loans, a staggering number totaling $445,000,000. Most of these credits provided housing for war workers. Few of the loans carried any risks for the bank: under Title VI of the Federal Housing Administration Act, that agency guaranteed them.

Branch banking proved to be eminently flexible in servicing this latest surge of California population and allowed A. P. to continue expansion of his system. In boom communities the bank often came under special strains. Wartime conditions created unusual problems. One was the necessity for the bank to provide change in coins to meet large payrolls and consumer demands. That required counting, packaging, and transporting coins by the ton. Bank of America branches that had handled between $10,000 and $15,000 daily before 1940 now had to cope with transactions totaling millions. Branches also extended their banking hours to serve the unprecedented flow of customers. On some days more than ten thousand people used the Richmond branch, for example, its deposits increasing from $2.5 million to $19 million.

A. P. also hoped to utilize this wartime surge of population to further the continued expansion of branch banking. In this he was to meet a certain measure of disappointment. The comptroller-general refused to approve all of his requests for opening new branches. Whether he liked it or not, A. P. had developed a reputation for having built a behemoth in the banking industry. Thus he was forced to consolidate some of his older branches and to transfer their charters to new units in areas of greatest need. The problems were particularly pressing near recently established military bases, which proliferated in California. Long lines at Bank of America branches near these installations became common. A. P. went on a tour to inspect such facilities in 1941 and was alarmed. Some 20,000 soldiers were encamped near San Luis Obispo, for example, a town of 9,000. Nearby Paso Robles, a community of 3,000, hosted another 20,000 GI's. When 100,000 troops went on maneuvers at the Hunter Liggett Military Reservation, they found the nearest bank in the town of King City, then a sleepy village of 1,800. Nevertheless, the comptroller-general refused A. P.'s requests for new branches, and the Bank of America emerged from the war in 1945 with three fewer units than it had in 1940. To sweeten A. P.'s disappointment slightly the Treasury Department awarded his bank a citation for distinguished service in view of his many contributions, including the sale of $2.7 billion of war bonds and other federal securities, more than any other private bank in the United States.

Although A. P. felt hemmed in by the reluctance of the Treasury Department to give him a carte blanche to multiply his branches further, he resorted to his legendary ingenuity to meet wartime needs. As he pondered alternatives, he remembered an obscure clause in the Banking Act of 1935 that allowed banks to establish seasonal agencies, as at state fairs or in tourist resorts. In March of 1942, when he first coyly inquired about the possibility of utilizing this provision, he received a rather negative response from Deputy Comptroller C. B. Upham. Quite bluntly Upham noted that he did not like "to see the Bank of America use the war as a means of expanding the number of its branches." Nevertheless, A. P. aggressively seized the opportunity rather than let his competitors win the new business. In May of 1942 he instructed his branch managers to provide banking services whenever military commanders requested them. Let the comptroller fight the military brass in wartime, A. P. reasoned! In addition, with the permission of the Federal Reserve Bank of San Francisco, he opened two branches in Japanese detention camps, at Tule Lake and at Lone Pine. Although the comptroller-general approved new branch banks in most states during the war years, he continued reluctant to authorize new outlets in California, either for the Bank of America or for any other bank there. He was convinced that branch banking was already overextended in the state. Still, A. P. succeeded in setting up fifty new de facto branches, which he described as "installations." Privately, he complained bitterly to Eccles at the Federal Reserve Board about what he considered as rank discrimination. Early in 1943 the Treasury Department bowed to the inevitable and gave its official approval to A. P.'s temporary outlets.

The war did much to accelerate the business of the bank. If A. P.

could not increase the number of his formal branches, he was able to double the number of deposits during these hectic years. These totaled almost $2 billion in 1941; by 1945 they had grown to $4.6 billion. Like much of the Pacific Coast and the Southwest, the Bank of America profited enormously from the wartime boom. In four years it doubled the scope of most of its operations. As a result, in 1945 A. P. witnessed the emergence of his institution as the world's largest bank.

Wartime conditions also brought social changes to the bank. During the conflict A. P. found it necessary to expand his staff as the demand for services increased. This was not easy because the bank sent 3,521 of its 9,765 employees to the armed forces. Yet by 1945 it took 11,677 people to operate his institution. The challenge was met by hiring women to replace the men who had left. By 1945 women composed one-half of the bank's employees, reflecting the growing percentage of females in the nation's work force.

The end of the war brought both hopes and fears to many business leaders in California and the West. The fears revolved around the expectation that the country might possibly return to the depression conditions of the 1930s. The hopes were that the war inaugurated a new era of prosperity for Americans such as they had never experienced. Among those who were hopeful were perennial optimists like Henry J. Kaiser and, of course, A. P. Both brimmed with great and exciting expectations about the future of the West. They applauded California's governor, Earl Warren, when he declared, in contemplating the future in 1945: "We have sniffed our destiny." A. P. was just as explicit. "The West Coast hasn't even started yet," he announced. Its further growth would provide jobs for everyone. "All the new inventions of wartime—electron[ic]s, television, light metals, products of every description," would be the basis of a better and more diversified economy in California, one in which agribusiness was balanced by a wide range of new industries and services. It would be an exciting and stimulating time.

Although A. P. was seventy-five years old in 1945, he continued to be a dreamer of big dreams. He could still become as excited as a schoolboy about the extraordinary opportunities for expansion that he saw all about him. The economic growth simulated by the war created enormous new fields of endeavors for his bank not only in California but throughout the entire West. Beyond these he envisaged a whole succession of new global challenges for the United

States and his bank. He had lived long enough to establish branch banking in California; he was still trying to achieve it on a national scale. And in reaching for still higher goals, he was considering the worldwide challenges, for was not branch banking feasible on a global scale?

Nevertheless, by 1945 age and infirmity were beginning to take their toll. On May 5, 1945, A. P. resigned his position as chairman of the board at the Bank of America. Although it was an aspect of his life that he loved dearly, he found it necessary to withdraw somewhat from the daily administrative affairs of the bank. This certainly did not end his influence in the institution's affairs. He continued to exercise a dominant voice in the shaping of all great decisions. His role now came to be that of an éminence grise—an interested observer, but not an active participant. His official title was "founder-chairman," and it gave him unchallenged status and power.

The enormous expansion of California in the postwar decade once more provided a context for A. P. that he relished. It created opportunities that his fertile brain found ripe for exploitation. A. P. and California were well matched. During the 1940s California gained 3,678,000 new residents and became the second largest state in the Union, after New York. Ebulliently A. P. predicted in 1945 that by 1960 it would overtake the eastern state. In such an expansionist environment the Bank of America made the most of its opportunities and sought to grow at an even faster rate than the state. From 1940 to 1950 it increased its capital from $62 million to $150 million, and deposits grew from $1.6 billion to $6.1 billion. A. P. waxed ecstatic. "Here is the heart of a great new empire," he declared in 1945, "an area of unbounded possibilities." Many of these he saw in housing and in the construction of new public utilities and new transportation facilities. Between 1945 and 1950 the Bank of America bought up more than one-half of the bonds issued by the state of California and sold them through its well-established mass marketing system. It also invested more money in municipal bonds than any other bank in the United States. This was especially significant for A. P. because now western banks like his own were able to supplant the large Wall Street institutions in financing western economic growth.

In addition, A. P. took advantage of federal programs to further his bank's expansion, as he had often done in the past. This was especially true in the sphere of housing. A. P. had already benefited for many years from the loan guarantees of the Federal Housing

Administration established under the New Deal. Now he derived even greater advantages from the GI Bill of Rights in 1944, under which Congress granted special benefits to war veterans. By 1949 the bank had extended $600 million in loans to World War II veterans under this act, more than 10 percent of the national total. Meanwhile, the bank was still developing the mass market in housing, financing seventy-eight thousand home loans between 1945 and 1952. Drawing on his World War II relationship with Henry J. Kaiser, A. P. granted more than $50 million in loans to Kaiser for building of six thousand Kaiser Community Homes in Los Angeles (Panorama City) and in San Jose. In San Francisco the bank lent even greater sums to Henry Doelger, a major developer there in the postwar era. A. P. also provided credit for a myriad of other Kaiser enterprises. He lent more than $25 million yearly to Kaiser for his ventures in aluminum, chemicals, cement, steel, and the justly famous Kaiser Health Plan, which built a great new health center in Oakland. Kaiser Steel received $11.5 million from the Bank of America in 1950 to expand its Fontana works, and $65 million in 1952 for a tinplate rolling mill. A. P. even supported Kaiser's plan to manufacture his Kaiser-Frazer automobiles in California and was disappointed when Kaiser could not resist the federal government's tempting offer of a low-cost lease on the giant Willow Run plant in Detroit. Even so, A. P. advised his bank to lend Kaiser $12 million to start the venture, sums it increased in ensuing years.

The buccaneering spirit of A. P. in forging his bank's further expansion between 1945 and 1949 continued to arouse the concern of federal regulators. His image as a monopolist, as a man who ruthlessly stamped out competition, would not die. Moreover, throughout his career federal and state regulators had found it difficult to contain the man. Whenever they sought to block him, he would find new loopholes by which he eluded them. In depression as in war, A. P. proved consistent in promoting the growth of his institution, quite irrespective of legal or bureaucratic barriers. By 1945 even Marriner Eccles—a lifelong friend of A. P. and staunch ally—began to have doubts about his ultimate goals and his seemingly insatiable appetite for expansion. Although between 1946 and 1949 the comptroller relented on the previous policy of rejecting all applications for branches, the pace was slow and cautious. From 1947 to 1949 A. P. was able to add only twenty-five new branches, most in the booming neighborhoods of Los Angeles.

Like many Americans in 1945, A. P. was greatly impressed by the new global perspectives that the war had inspired among Americans. In his case, the war whetted his desire to expand his bank's worldwide operations. As the son of immigrants, he had been sensitive to foreign influences all his life. From his first beginnings as a banker, he had handled a higher percentage of foreign remittances than most other American bankers. By the end of World War I he had purchased his first Italian branch and in 1931 another one in London. The depression obviously placed a damper on the expansion of these operations. But in 1945 the situation was different. In October of that year A. P. flew to Europe to inspect his Italian bank and to survey the need for reconstruction. Greatly impressed by the need for American capital in the task of rebuilding, he poured large sums into his Italian bank and its Italian affiliates. Within eighteen months he made $37 million available in lines of credit to rejuvenate imports and exports. His activities received plaudits from administration officials in Washington. "The president [Truman] and I are pleased," wrote John W. Snyder, director of the Office of War Mobilization and Conversion, to A. P. in December 1945. "I regard this type of action as a positive contribution to worldwide recovery." During the next four years A. P. undertook international expansion with the same aggressiveness with which he had built his bank at home. In addition to establishing new branches in Europe, he also created new ones in the Pacific, which he viewed as the next great area for economic development on a large scale.

Although partially retired, A. P. was able to imbue many of his staff with the exhilaration that many westerners felt in 1945, a feeling that their days of virtual colonial dependence on the financially more mature East were ended. At the Bank of America many of its executives now felt that the establishment of global banking was no longer the sole prerogative of Wall Street bankers. "We don't like to see exports from San Francisco financed by New York lines of credit," Mario Giannini announced at a director's meeting on April 29, 1949. "We expect to build the position of the Bank of America in the international field to a point where it will be comparable to the bank's position in the domestic field. We feel we owe it to the country, to our state, to our customers, and to the stockholders."

For the first time, therefore, A. P. and his associates planned expansion into the Pacific. In January 1946 the Gianninis were jolted by a letter they received from Frank Belgrano, on leave from their Central

Bank in Oakland to serve as financial adviser to Paul W. McNutt, the U.S. High Commissioner to the Philippines. "At the moment everything is needed here," he wrote. "The immediate future seems to me to hold great possibilities if the right sort of concerns are properly financed." A. P. immediately sent a representative to the area to assess its potentials. He recommended the opening of a branch in Manila. Authority for establishment of such branches rested with the Federal Reserve Board in Washington, where A. P.'s friend Marriner Eccles was still chairman. Eccles secured rapid approval, and in January 1947 the Manila branch became A. P.'s first Pacific venture. In only a few years it made itself one of the leading financial institutions in the Islands.

From the Philippines A. P.'s assistants went to the Asian mainland. Shortly before the Communists took over China, the Bank of America established a branch in Shanghai. That was obviously a bad move, since the Communist government quickly closed it down when it captured the city. But a new branch in Bankok, Thailand, in 1949 gave the Bank of America a foothold in Southeast Asia. Another great success was a new facility in Guam. But probably the most profitable new area for operations was Japan. There the Bank of America opened four new branches between 1947 and 1952. Located in major business centers such as Tokyo, Yokohama, Kobe, and Osaka, they provided A. P. with a major base for his Far Eastern operations. And to A. P.'s great satisfaction, it established his bank's parity—and even leadership—with the older and conservative New York banks, who were slower to enter what was still an uncertain market.

In entering world markets, A. P. took full advantage of government postwar reconstruction programs. Under the Marshall Plan, the U.S. government gave Western European nations generous economic aid, but one-fifth of these grants were in loans that were to be repaid. The federal government allowed each country to select the private bank with which it could deal. Older established institutions like Chase National Bank of New York obviously had an advantage, since they were well known to Europeans. Indeed, these were the most popular choices. But A. P. was proud of the fact that his Bank of America was sixth in the amount of loans made. And he took special pride in the role of the Bank of America in Italian reconstruction, where it was the leader in terms of the total funds provided. One of the bank's chief farm experts, Harry McClelland, became chief of the

Economic Cooperation Administration's Italian mission. McClelland utilized funds to modernize Italian agriculture through drainage programs and mechanization. Although A. P. did not live to see it in his lifetime, within a year of his death the Bank of America established a new international division. With offices in New York, it was designed to compete with Wall Street institutions in penetrating European markets.

A. P.'s retirement years saw some of the most spectacular growth of the Bank of America in both domestic and global markets. His genius then—as in earlier years—was to recognize opportunities and then to utilize his administrative skills to build upon them. These opportunities he quite rightly saw in the dynamic growth potentials of California, the West, and in a myriad of federal programs that he used to his advantage. At the same time, his vision embraced the entire world, as he foresaw American penetration of Europe, and especially the Pacific. In all of these ventures he retained a soft spot in his heart for the little person. Clearly, he was not primarily a philanthropist but a hard-headed businessman. But his special insight was to transform his understanding of the common person into the exploitation of consumer-oriented mass markets and diversified economies, here and abroad. A. P. perceived these potentials long before many other bankers did. And World War II and the postwar era created conditions within which he was able to realize even his more optimistic dreams.

In 1945 A. P. retired as chairman of the board of directors at the Bank of America. At the same time, his perceived adversary, Henry L. Morgenthau, Jr., left his post as secretary of the treasury. But the controversy over A. P.'s monopolistic tendencies continued. Beginning in 1948, the Federal Reserve Board inaugurated an investigation of the Transamerica Corporation, charging that it violated an antimonopoly clause of the Clayton Act of 1914. Hearings on the issue extended over the next three years, culminating in a board order requiring TransAmerica to divest itself of all stocks except those it held in the Bank of America.

A. P. did not live to witness the resolution of the controversy. His last public appearance was on April 28, 1949, when he attended the annual meeting of Transamerica Corporation stockholders. Within a week thereafter he found himself suffering from a bad cold. On his birthday, May 6, he was too uncomfortable and hoarse to work at his desk at the bank's San Francisco headquarters. Soon thereafter his doctors directed him to St. Luke's Hospital in San Francisco, where he remained for one week. But he was a very restless patient and decided to go home to more familiar surroundings in San Mateo. Unfortunately, his condition worsened, and his doctors placed him in Mills General Hospital, where he was confined to an oxygen tent. After seeming improvement, his doctors released him on Saturday, May 28, as A. P. expected to be back at the bank within a week. But that was not to be. On June 3, 1949, he died in his sleep, victim of a heart attack and arterial sclerosis. Some of his closest family members had preceded him in death. His son Virgil had passed away in 1938, and his beloved wife, Clorinda, three years later. Surviving A. P. was his son Mario, president of the Bank of America, and his daughter, Claire Giannini Hoffman, who took his seat on the bank's board of directors.

For a man of his eminence, A. P. left a very modest estate. As he was reported to have said in 1946: "Why should a man pile a lot of money for somebody to spend after he's gone?" When he retired in 1945, he established the Bank of America–Giannini Foundation. He endowed it with a gift of $509,235, about one-half of his personal fortune, and instructed it to support medical research and to provide scholarships for Bank of America employees. His will in 1949 directed that most of the remainder of his fortune, $439,278, be given to the foundation.

A. P. was widely mourned. On Monday morning, June 6, 1949, Archbishop John J. Mitty conducted a requiem mass for A. P., a lifelong Roman Catholic, at St. Mary's Cathedral in San Francisco. A large crowd gathered to pay their respects to one of California's best-known citizens. He was buried in Holy Cross Cemetery in Coloma, not far from his home. At the University of California, where A. P. had been a benefactor as well as a regent, President Gordon Sproul ordered flags flown at half mast. In keeping with A. P.'s wishes, all branches of the Bank of America remained open on the day of his funeral.

When A. P. died, he left behind the world's largest bank, with 517 branches and more than $6 billion in assets. He had built the institution from scratch. As J. P. Morgan had personified banking for the wealthy classes, so A. P. symbolized banking for the masses. One could argue whether A. P. was an autocrat or a democrat, for he embodied both of these characteristics. What is less arguable is that he succeeded in fulfilling his dream of building a bank used by

common people. As he told his executives upon his retirement in
1945: "If I ever hear that any of you are trying to play the big man's
game and forgetting the small man, I'll be back in here fighting." It
was this spirit that imbued the Bank of America with a dynamism
during his lifetime that other bankers found hard to match.

Conclusion: A. P. in Retrospect

A. P. was one of the most successful bankers of his generation. That success was due to various factors. Some of it was related to his entrepreneurial talents. He had a boundless capacity for innovation, for imagination and vision, limned by a capacity for hard work. He himself as well as others regarded him as an outstanding example of the American success story, a son of immigrants who fought and clawed his way to eminence in his chosen field. His enormous drive and ambition were oriented not so much to the accumulation of wealth as to self-fulfillment and the exercise of power. At the same time, he had managerial skills of a high order. He had a clear grasp of the relation between centralization and decentralization, and of subtleties in the exercise of authority. His ability to motivate his staff through a complex system of rewards and punishments was impressive. He was a benevolent leader as well as a harsh taskmaster. All of these traits reflected his insight into human nature, his effectiveness as a communicator, and his grasp of the importance of image. Together, his entrepreneurial and managerial skills made him an outstanding chief executive who was able to attain many of his goals, despite serious obstacles.

His entrepreneurial talents were many. He relished the founding of new enterprises and made this one of his central goals. The commission business of his youth did not provide sufficient scope for his large ambitions, but he found that banking provided him with far broader outlets for his restless energies. Branch banking seemed particularly well suited to his personality, for the extension of branches in the state, then the region, after that the nation, and then the world provided unlimited challenges and possibilities. In pursuit of these ambitions he was fortunate throughout much of his life because economic conditions were propitious. The Great Depression provided the first serious impediment to his single-minded campaigns. Thereafter his image as a ruthless power broker and would-be monopolist created opposition not only within the banking profession but among government regulators as well. Yet if obstacles slowed his pace, they did not seriously impede his relentless drive to build the largest banking institution in the world.

His insights into human nature were outstanding. A. P. never undertook the formal study of psychology, but he was expert in manipulating the behavior of others. His powers of persuasion were legendary. He was gregarious and outgoing. His liking for people was genuine. That led him to stress accessibility and openness, not only in his own demeanor, but in that of his employees and associates. His banks thus provided a friendly, informal, and open atmosphere. From the time he hired his first staff in 1904 at the Bank of Italy to his last year at the Bank of America, he made sure that the institution reflected this aspect of his personality.

His imagination transcended that of most other bankers of his day. His own sense of innovation usually characterized the policies of the banks he founded. In his first decade as a banker, he introduced long banking hours, emphasized savings deposits, and pioneered in the extension of small and low-cost loans. In his second decade in the profession he successfully sought out new industries such as motion pictures, aggressively developed the technique of branch banking, and kept pace with California's urban expansion. In the 1930s he branched out actively into new spheres such as auto and consumer financing, business advisement, and the organization of special divisions to cater to specific ethnic and racial minorities. And in his last decade he took pride in participation in syndicates and in global expansion. His bank was certainly not the only one to provide such services, but he did much as a pioneer to develop them more fully.

A. P.'s capacities as a manager equaled his prowess as an enterpriser. The development of branch banking could be likened to the development of mass production techniques in the realm of industry by such of his contemporaries as Henry Ford. A. P. realized the efficiency of large-scale operation that could tap a mass market in ways which small, independent bankers rarely could. Like the chain stores and mass merchandisers of his day, A. P. developed a department-store approach to the field, which was a novel innovation.

A. P. also possessed artful political skills. He was as much a businessman in politics as he was a politician in business. During much of his life he resorted to political leverage to advance his business. His entry into politics was varied. At times, as in the California gubernatorial race of 1926, it was direct. At other times he manipulated the business-government complex. It was his practice to hire well-known politicians at the bank, often as legal counsel or consultants, usually in relation to the same public agencies in which they had served. Thus he hired former State Banking Superintendent William A. Williams to negotiate with his successors. When he met resistance from the Federal Reserve Board in 1923, he retained a former secretary of the treasury, William McAdoo. And when he faced difficulties with the Justice Department in 1937 on antitrust actions, he brought Donald Richberg into the fold, a former director of the National Recovery Administration.

He was also adept in lobbying. His behind-the-scenes negotiations facilitated a favorable entry into the Federal Reserve System for his banks in the era after World War I. His lobbyists secured especially advantageous terms for his national banks in the McFadden Act of 1927. That experience stood him in good stead during the banking crisis of 1933, when, despite the emergency, he wrested terms from Congress in the Banking Acts of 1933 and 1935 that dispensed special favors to his bank. So successful was his lobbying that after 1935 his fame aroused increasing opposition.

More than most bankers, A. P. was extremely conscious of his public image. Early in his career he broke precedent by resorting to techniques disdained by others. He embraced advertising with enthusiasm, utilizing newspapers, radio, and billboards. Eager to tell the world about the services he could offer, he saw nothing wrong with intensive personal solicitation. If he was to attract other people's money, he realized clearly, he had to set out to win their confidence and imbue them with a feeling of security. From his days as a commission merchant until old age, he sought to reflect an image of integrity and fairness. Despite his innovativeness, he also exuded an aura of conservatism, one that stood him in good stead especially with immigrants, who were particularly suspicious in a foreign land.

His capacity for hard work was legendary. To him the long hours he spent at the bank were not work in the sense of drudgery, but pure enjoyment. In his youth, days of working twelve to eighteen hours on the docks or in traversing the great valleys of California were common. His regimen was no less demanding as a banker. As his health deteriorated in the later 1920s, his pace slackened as he sought relief from painful neuritis in European spas. Although away from the bank for months, he still kept in daily touch. Few of his associates at the beginning of the 1930s believed he could continue on a full-time basis. But the economic crisis seemed to rejuvenate him. As he attempted to nurse his ailing bank back to health, he reverted to his former eighteen-hour day and, surprising everyone, regained much of his former stamina.

In many ways the Bank of America became an extension of his personality. To A. P. it was *la famiglia,* a big family embracing employees, stockholders, and depositors. He presided over it like a benevolent patriarch. The orientation of the bank to average people, its informality and simplicity, the courtesy extended by the staff, and a bevy of consulting services available to clients all reflected A. P.'s belief in service to the multitudes. Having worked with farmers and small-business people, A. P. was well aware of their needs and their orientation. Helping them with their special problems not only gave him great satisfaction but was good business as well.

A. P. was very much a product of the West. He could not have cut the image of a banker from Boston, New York, or Philadelphia. In so many ways he reflected not only his own times but the region in which he was born and in which he lived a lifetime. His belief in growth, in unlimited opportunities, in diversity, and in innovation and experimentation were all implicit or explicit assumptions of most westerners between 1870 and 1950. A. P. capitalized on them, utilized them, and built his bank upon them. These were the assumptions of his contemporaries. The West provided the arena in which he could apply his talents to an unusual degree. California and the West provided the opportunities that A. P. could exploit; in turn, he developed an institution that significantly affected the development of the region that he loved so well.

A Note on Sources

THE most extensive collection of A. P.'s correspondence is found in the Bank of America archives in San Francisco. Letters quoted in this volume, with names and dates, are deposited in the Bank of America Archives. The materials were gathered there between 1947 and 1952 by Marquis and Bessie James, whom bank officials had authorized to write a detailed history of the institution. Employing a large staff, they also conducted scores of interviews with A. P. and the individuals who were associated with him. Transcripts were deposited in the archives. Although the Bank of America archives are voluminous, they need to be supplemented by other sources. Since A. P. had such extensive contacts, a wide range of manuscript collections contain materials relating to him. These include the papers of U.S. presidents such as Calvin Coolidge materials at the Library of Congress, Herbert Hoover at the Hoover Presidential Library, and Franklin D. Roosevelt's associates at the Roosevelt Presidential Library at Hyde Park. The records of the Federal Reserve Board in Washington, D.C., of the U.S. comptroller-general, and of the Reconstruction Finance Corporation contain significant numbers of A. P.'s letters. This is also true of correspondence in collections of the Federal Reserve Bank of San Francisco and manuscript collections of individuals such as Marriner Eccles, Jesse Jones, and Henry L. Morgenthau, Jr. Nor should vast holdings in California be ignored, especially records of the State Banking Department.

Newspapers and magazines contain a great deal of information about A. P. Those in San Francisco, Los Angeles, and Sacramento are the most useful. The Bank of Italy's house organ, *Bankitaly Life* (and its successors) is indispensable. *L'Italia*, San Francisco's leading Italian-language newspaper, is especially informative for the period before World War I. The files of the *Coast Banker*, reporting on the industry on the Pacific Coast, are chock-full of information. Interviews with A. P. can be found in *Forbes*, November 10, 1923; *Personnel Efficiency*, January 11, 1925; *Wall Street Journal*, June 21, 1925; *San Francisco Chronicle*, February 23, 1927; *San Francisco Examiner*, May 23, 1927, and August 1, 1941; and *Sacramento Bee*, January 2, 1936.

A full-scale biography of A. P. still needs to be written. Julian P. Dana, who wrote the first authorized biography and interviewed A. P. at length, provided an adulatory portrait in *A. P. Giannini: Giant in the West* (New York, 1947). Then followed Marquis and Bessie James, *Biography of a Bank* (New York, 1954), which, as its title indicates, was intended to be a history of the institution, not the life story of its founder. Sponsored by bank officials, it is an excellent work with extensive notes. One aspect of A. P.'s activities was subjected to close scrutiny in a doctoral dissertation by Russel M. Posner, "State Politics and the Bank of America, 1920–1934" (University of California, Berkeley, 1957). Julian Dana took extensive notes on his interviews with A. P., and these can be consulted in the Julian Dana Papers in the Bancroft Library at the University of California. Studies of the Bank of America after A. P.'s death that allude to his influence include Gary Hector, *Breaking the Bank: The Decline of Bankamerica* (Boston, 1988), and Moira Johnson, *Roller Coaster: The Bank of America and the Future of American Banking* (New York, 1990).

Oral histories of Californians who knew A. P. can be found in the excellent collections of the University of California Oral History Program, Berkeley. Interviews with Thomas Crowley, William Figari, and Russel Smith serve as examples of the value of this type of source.

To place A. P. in the context of his generation, several works on Italians in California are useful. Andrew Rolle, *The Immigrant Upraised* (Norman, Okla., 1968), Deanna Paoli, *The Italians of San Francisco, 1850–1930* (New York, 1978), and Dino Cinel, *Conservative Adventurers: The Italian Migrants in Italy and San Francisco* (Palo Alto, Calif., 1982), provide this dimension.

A. P. was a favorite subject for many journalists. Among the many articles that can be consulted are Pauline Jacobson, "How I Began Life: Amadeo P. Giannini Tells Pauline Jacobson," *San Francisco Call,* November 8, 1921, and articles in *San Francisco Examiner,* May 24, 1924, and *San Francisco Chronicle,* February 28, 1927, and *Look,* "A. P. Giannini: Banker to the West," May 1927. A very informative seven-part series was written by Reed Hayes, entitled "A Real Romance of San Francisco: The Story of the Bank of Italy and A. P. Giannini," in the *San Francisco News,* starting March 6, 1928. Outstanding also is a four-part series by the well-known Matthew Josephson in the *Saturday Evening Post,* beginning with the September 1947 issue. Jane Conant contributed essays in the *San Francisco Call Bulletin* on June 3, and 6, 1949.

A. P.'s relationship with his brother Attilio can be discerned in various publications by and about this perennially frustrated man. These include his own writings such as "Financing the Production and Distribution of Motion Pictures," *Annals of the American Academy of Social and Political Science* 128 (November 1926): 45–50, and a chapter he contributed to *The Story of the Films,* ed. Joseph P. Kennedy (Chicago, 1927). See also newspaper articles about him in

San Francisco Examiner, October 7, 1927 and February 8, 1943; *San Francisco Call,* October 17, 1927; *New York Times,* October 30, 1927; *Wall Street Journal,* September 10, 1935; and *San Francisco Chronicle,* December 6, 1936. Informative is Frank Taylor, "He's No Angel," *Saturday Evening Post,* January 14 1939.

Index